Swim School Success

Swim School Success

Lane Harrison

CONTENTS

CONTENTS

CONTENTS

Welcome To Swim School Success

In this book, I'll be sharing with you, ideas, strategies, and frameworks that will help you grow your swim school

I will teach you new ideas on how to acquire more customers, improve your conversion rates, increase member satisfaction, and improve retention rates.

The reason I wrote this book is that I love helping businesses grow and improve.

The strategies in this book are dynamite yet are not being implemented by a lot of the industry.

I will also be sharing with you not only my thoughts and strategies but the thoughts of many of the industry's leading operators.

If you implement the ideas in this book, you can leapfrog your competition and enjoy more profits and more satisfaction.

It's important to acknowledge that competition within the industry is at an all-time high.

Besides that, swim school owners and managers are becoming savvier.

Once, swim school owners were more technical based.

In other words, they knew the technical aspects of running a swim school, like, how to roster staff, how to write a lesson plan, how to teach, etc.

But the success of a swim school is more about understanding business systems and processes, like, marketing, retention, and technology.

Don't get me wrong, understanding all the technical elements of running a swim school are still important- you just can't afford to neglect the areas that drive business growth.

So, with the increased competition, and the increased business skills of swim school owners and managers, you can no longer be average to survive and thrive, you need to be at the top of your game.

That's what this book is designed to do...

To share with you the best practices and most effective strategies for acquiring and retaining customers.

I encourage you to think of your swim school as a big system made up of smaller subsystems.

What's awesome is you can install new systems or new sub-systems into that overall system. So, for example, you might install a new system (process) for generating leads or you might install a system for improving customer retention.

If you take a system or process that has been proven to work and implement it in your swim school, you're likely to get similar results.

Swim school success will teach you the systems and processes proven to grow swim school profits.

We will focus on 5 subsystems or business units throughout the book. These are....

1. A traffic system. (How do we generate leads)
2. A conversion system (How do we convert those leads)
3. An onboarding system. (How do we get new customers started)
4. A retention/customer success system. (How do we ensure we retain our customers)
5. An operational system (team, systems, etc)

We'll be going deep with each of those areas in the book. So, strap yourself in because you're about to learn some exciting new ideas to grow your swim school business.

2 |

Who Am I And Why Should You Take The Time To Read This Book?

Before we get started, I'll quickly explain a little bit about my background.

Why am I writing this book and why am I qualified to write it?

My journey in the Aquatic and Recreation industry started in 2007.

In the early 2000s, after finishing high school, I was an athlete, doing track and field. And I was training full time hoping to become a professional athlete, and hopefully make the Olympic Games.

This dream ended in 2006 when an Achilles injury meant that I could no longer compete and train at the level required.

So, I was stuck without a plan.

I thought about my future and what I wanted to do and passed the time by completing a personal training/gym instructor course.

I'd spent a lot of time during my athletics career in the gym. I knew how to do weights and create programs. I'd done strength and conditioning courses, so a gym instructor course felt like a natural progression.

After qualifying as a gym instructor, I started my own business.

The business involved managing gyms for private schools in Victoria. We managed gyms for about eight major private schools, and I eventually sold that business.

I then moved on to developing and being part of a software start-up for the Aquatic and Recreation industry, which focused on gym programming and retention.

We grew this software company from the ground up, with no capital. We put $10,000 on a credit card to go to our first trade show in Sydney.

It took us 12 months to acquire our first customer; it was a painful experience. We struggled to gain traction and I was left searching for answers and help.

During this period, I would read a different business book each week, an investment that helped me considerably.

After 12 months, we were lucky enough to slowly build up a successful business in this space.

One customer became two, two became four, four became dozens, and eventually, we had hundreds of customers using our software solutions.

In 2014 some of our customers in the Aquatic and Recreation industry discussed some of their needs relating to managing their swim schools.

This led to the development of our well known SwimDesk software that is used by hundreds of swim schools across Australia, New Zealand and now 4 other countries.

Through that, I worked directly with a lot of swim school owners and managers, not only implementing our software but helping them implement business processes and best practices that would help them retain more customers and increase their revenues and profits.

What I learnt from books and courses I would implement in both our business as well as in the businesses of our clients.

Today, I've worked directly with hundreds of swim schools, and have been refining the processes and frameworks we use with our clients to maximize their results.

Over the past 7 years, I have conducted dozens of educational webinars, workshops and online training sessions on the topic of swim school growth.

I am also the host of a podcast focused on helping swim schools grow- The Swim School Business Podcast.

Now, one thing to note is that I've never actually owned my private swim school.

So, you could say that maybe I'm not qualified to speak or write about optimising and maximising profits in a swim school.

Yes, I may not have the experience of owning my swim school; however, it's important to understand that maximizing the profits of a swim school is more about understanding processes and best practices around things like marketing, sales. customer success, retention, etc., rather than knowing how to teach swimming strokes.

Renowned business and marketing expert Jay Abraham often talks about the value of taking successful ideas and processes from other industries and using them in your industry.

My unique experience of working deeply with swim schools as well as building my own software business allows me to take concepts that work in one and apply them to the other.

So that's enough about me. I'm excited to share with you the ideas in this book, so let's not waste any more time. Let's get into it and start growing your swim school.

3

The 3 Biggest Mistakes Swim School's Make That Limit Growth And Profits

A swim school can be an amazing and profitable business when successful. However, reaching success takes a lot of hard work, perseverance, and avoidance of critical mistakes.

Let's get started by exploring the three biggest mistakes swim school managers make that limit growth and profitability.

Mistake 1- Failure to work *"on"* the business

The famous business book the *E Myth* by Michael Gerber states that business owners should spend more time working *"on"* the business rather than in the business. This concept is true in every industry. Many business owners and managers spend far too much time working in the business rather than *"on the business"*.

I see this time and time again in the swim school industry, where managers will be running group swim school classes or training clients. In some ways, this could be seen as positive. That the manager isn't afraid to roll their sleeves up; however, it often means time is being invested in the wrong areas.

Many managers and owners start as trainers or swim school instructors. And slowly make their way up to the point of being a manager or perhaps decided they want to go out on their own and open their facility. They rationalise that they know how a swim school runs (they do). They know all the technical elements of running a swim school, from managing rosters, to teaching and even equipment maintenance.

The reality is running a successful swim school is more about understanding business skills such as marketing, sales, customer management and finance rather than the technical elements.

Focusing on these areas is *"working on"* the business and is where most managers or owners' attention should go.

Mistake 2 – Failure to understand the mechanics of the customer business model

Most swim schools are based on membership or a recurring business model.

This is a beautiful business model when done right due to its foundation of recurring revenue.

Essentially a swim school is one big business system made up of several subsystems.

If we boil things down to their simplest form, then there are only two key elements (key systems) of running a successful swim school

- Member acquisition
- Member retention

Everything else matters very little.

Peter Drucker, the legendary management guru, said, *"The purpose of business is to create and keep a customer."* If you want your business to grow, it's critical to keep your existing customers happy and add on new ones

The more you optimise these areas, the more profitable your swim school will be.

Many swim school managers and owners invest only a little time and energy each month into these areas.

This brings us to the two most important metrics in your swim school.

1. Cost to acquire a member

To be profitable, you must be able to acquire customers cost-effectively. Any dummy could spend 1 million dollars each month on advertising and bring in a bunch of new customers.

However, they would be losing buckets of money to acquire those customers. The better your marketing and sales conversion processes, the lower your cost to acquire a member will be.

2. The average length of stay (or customer lifetime value)

Member retention is everything in a customer business model. As your competition grows, it becomes harder and harder to acquire new customers cost-effectively. If you churn through most of your customer base every 12 months, you will find yourself on a sinking ship. Almost every swim school under invests in member retention!

If your swim school isn't tracking these two metrics, you are driving blind and will struggle to maximise your chances of success.

Mistake 3 – Failure to copy proven systems

Learning through trial and error can be a long and expensive process.

Learning through mistakes can be positive; however, sometimes, we do not have the luxury of making too many mistakes. Too many mistakes can lead to the competition getting the edge or our customer declining too much to sustain profitability.

A swim school can be seen as one big system made up of several smaller subsystems.

For example, generating leads for your swim school is done through a lead generation or traffic system.

The good thing about systems is that they typically can be copied and successfully transplanted.

If you can identify systems or processes already working for other swim schools or in other industries, you can *"model"* that system in your swim school and expect similar results.

Identifying a proven system you can model and implement in your swim school is the closest thing to a shortcut there is in business.

I do not believe there are *"magic bullets"* in business; success takes a lot of hard work, ongoing improvement and persistence. However, identifying successful systems you can model, can help you reach your target destination a lot faster than via the trial and error process.

4

The Swim School Growth Model

Before we get into the nitty-gritty of growing your swim school it is important to understand the core levers you can improve to increase your enrolment base and grow your revenues.

Introducing the swim school growth formula...

Customer Acquisition x Customer Retention x Ave Customer Value = Revenue Growth

This formula looks at the key variables that drive swim school revenue growth.

(Kinda like an old school mathematical formula from high school)

A swim school acquires 40 new customers in March

And has attrition (number of customers lost) of 30 customers

And the average monthly customer value is $80

This would tell us that the swim school has a net 10 student gain for the month and has increased its baseline recurring revenue from the previous month by $800.00

If you are acquiring more customers then you are losing your enrolment base should be increasing each month, however, if you are losing more customers than you are acquiring your enrolment base will be decreasing.

That's why it's important to keep track of these numbers.

- What is your customer acquisition?
- What is your customer attrition (number of customers lost)?
- What is your month starting enrolment count?

These metrics are like the GPS in your car, you should regularly check them to ensure you aren't heading in the wrong direction.

We can also break down these metrics further.

For example - Customer Acquisition can be broken down into two parts

1. Traffic (the number of leads your get)
2. Conversion (how many of those leads convert to sales

It's important to focus on these two areas when it comes to improving customer acquisition. We will be sharing a heap of strategies later in the book to help you with this.

The most exciting part of the swim school growth formula is that it gives you multiple areas where you can improve your business. If you can improve multiple of these areas simultaneously it can have a significant impact on your overall results.

Let's break down an example

Customer Acquisition (Traffic x Conversion) x Customer Retention x Ave customer value

Current performance

Customer Acquisition

Traffic 60 leads conversion 35%- =21 new customers

Customer Retention= 15 customer lost

Ave customer value- $80 per month

Net gain - 6 x $80= $480 in revenue growth

Now lets look at a scenario where we improve by these key areas each by 15%

Traffic= 69 leads

Conversion 50% - 34 new customers (rounded down)

Customer Retention - 12 customers lost

Average customer value $92 per month

Net gain= 22 x 92 = $2024 revenue gain

By improving each variable in the overall formula by 15% we have seen the revenue gain more than quadruple.

This is the compounding power of improving each area of the formula.

To be fair 15% is a big jump in each of these metrics- however, if you can improve each area by at least 5% by focusing on implementing proven and successful strategies you can expect to see a total transformation of your business results.

The exciting news is that these improvements have an even greater compounding effect over the long term and can result in hundreds of thousands of extra revenues each year.

5

7 Must-Have Marketing Channels You Should Develop And Optimise In Your Swim Schools

The worst number in business is one. This particularly applies to your marketing. If you are dependent on one marketing channel for the bulk of your leads and that channel stops working you leave yourself in a precarious position.

That's why it's important to have a multi-channel approach to your marketing efforts.

Below are 7 must-have marketing channels that every swim school should focus on.

Google ads

Where do many people start when considering joining a swim school? Often by googling "swim schools in their suburb". You must have ads that relate to those search terms. Ideally, you should be listed first for these key searches, if not first, you want to be in the top 3. Competitors can always increase their bids for these searches, so it's important to keep an eye on where your ads place in the search.

Facebook/Instagram ads

Where do most people spend their spare time? On social media, of course. (Perhaps unfortunately but we will leave that discussion for another day). Lead generation through social media advertising is a strong medium that every swim school should have in play.

Target your local and surrounding area in your advertising tightly. The best advertising has a clear call to action, and you should attempt to capture the lead's contact information. (More on this later). You can do this by offering a bribe such as downloading a free trial swim or some valuable information- Eg. 10 things to consider before choosing a swim school for your child.

Email marketing

Some people have said email is dead, but they are wrong. When done right, email is perhaps the most powerful tool at your disposal to generate interest and stimulate action. The key to good email marketing is giving value. You must provide value in good and engaging content.

Many swim school owners make the mistake of only using email to promote a special offer or sale. People quickly turn off this type of messaging and unsubscribe from your list.

However, if your email content is engaging and useful, then people will be more likely to read it. The right balance for your email marketing should be around 80% valuable content with 20% promotion/offers.

You should always be building your email list by having multiple ways to capture prospects contact information on your website.

Remarketing

Have you ever been in the middle of something and then got distracted and completely forget about what you were originally doing? This happens to me all the time.

We live in an interrupted society. Our phones and notifications are always going off, which can be a great distraction. This happens to your leads as well. They may be on your website and considering signing up for a free trial lesson for their child, and an important email pops up on their screen or their phone rings. Luckily there is a way to re-engage leads who have been on your website without acting.

By installing a remarketing pixel (a little bit of code) on your website, you can show ads to people who have visited your website on Facebook and other ad platforms, including the Google Display network. This is a powerful way of marketing because you are targeting those who have engaged with you in some way. You can even remarket to people who visited specific pages. (Such as prospects that have been on your contact us page or FAQ page).

Affiliates

Affiliate marketing has been around for ages, and that's because it works. Affiliate marketing is where you team up with other complementary local businesses to work together to share leads or promote each other. For example, you might team up with a local sports store that can send out a special promotion to their member database, and you can assist them by including a special offer for their store in your member welcome packs.

Another great option for swim schools is to affiliate with local schools to help get your business featured in their newsletter.

Offer to write them an educational article on water safety that they can include in their newsletter. (If it's educational and relevant for parents many will publish this content for free)

This is a simple example, but when done right, affiliate marketing can be very powerful.

The biggest mistake people make with affiliate marketing is that they are too focused on themselves. You need to create value for the other side. If you create a heap of value for affiliate partners, they will feel a sense of reciprocity and work harder to promote your business.

The best way to leverage affiliates is to think about who else has your customers and who else might have an email database of those customers. Then come up with a special piece of valuable content that your affiliate can email out to their list.

Referrals

Referrals are an underutilised medium for marketing a swim school.

The key is to ASK - If you wait in the hope, you won't generate nearly as many referrals are you can.

A great place to ask is when someone has joined for a trial lesson. Many swim schools have developed a phone script for trial lessons that ask the parent would their son/daughter like to bring a friend along for the trial swim.

This can instantly increase the number of lead opportunities at your disposal.

Another great time to ask for referrals is within the first 2 weeks of a customer joining.

Many swim schools that we work with include this within their onboarding processes.

Past customers

When we look at our client's data in terms of lead sources, it's always interesting to see that a large percentage of leads are past customers returning.

A lot of swim schools have no formalised marketing systems or processes for past customers. Do you have a "re-activation campaign" do you stay in front of your past customers and maintain top of mind awareness?

An easy way to do this is via a newsletter. You can easily create a monthly e-newsletter that contains educational content such as tips on water safety, or how to use swimming to improve fitness. This can help you stay in front of your past customers and continue to build value and goodwill. Then when you present an offer to them to re-join, they will be more receptive and more likely to act.

If you master the 7 areas of the lead generation above the engine of your customer acquisition process will be robust. The key is compounding your results by focusing on multiple lead generation pillars.

6

Using Principles Of Influence To Improve Your Sales Conversion

If you want to quickly learn how to improve your sales conversion, you need to understand how influence works. If you can understand what "triggers" people to make a decision you can take intelligent action to improve your levels of success.

The best resource to fast track your understanding of influence is the book- Influence by Robert Cialdini. This is considered a classic book on the psychology of influence, and I have found it to be invaluable.

Below is a quick summary of the 6 core principles of influence uncovered in the book.

1. Reciprocity
2. Scarcity
3. Authority
4. Consistency
5. Liking
6. Consensus

Let's unpack each of these and relate them to how we could use them in a swim school.

What is reciprocity?

If a friend invites you to their party, you feel an obligation to invite them to a future party you are hosting. People feel obliged to return a favour. If you give something of value to someone, they feel a need to repay that favour.

This principle can be used in our marketing efforts by giving a prospective customer a useful or educational resource. Something with genuine value. It might be an insightful article or short video course on how to improve your child's water safety skills. By giving value upfront, you build up some goodwill with your prospects, which can help boost your conversion.

We do this in our software business. We publish a lot of useful content that is completely free.

The quality of the information we provide is so good we could charge for it, but we give this away to help and provide upfront value for our potential customers. I think it's important to not expect anything in return. The goal should be to provide something of value, and if this helps someone, then they may be more receptive to working with you on a deeper level.

Scarcity

Rare things typically have a higher perceived value. Scarcity is often used to drive people to action. It can be in the form of a limited time offer or sale.

Sometimes using scarcity can be overdone and can turn people off. If you always have a special offer that must end on a certain date, people become immune to it.

I am a fan of using scarcity linked to a prospect's initial enquiry. For example, if someone is completing a trial lesson at your swim school, you could present an offer that expires within 3 days after their lesson. Eg. They get a pair of extra Google at half price if they enrol or you waive the normal joining fee.

Authority

People follow the lead of credible experts.

A person is more likely to listen to a nutritionist about dietary advice rather than some random person.

Our influence will increase if we are perceived as experts in a specific area.

Some ways to increase authority include writing articles, publishing small books, doing webinars, doing interviews, etc.

The key is to publish some content relevant to your prospects, and you will automatically be considered an expert.

There are countless ways to subtly display your expertise. Has your swim school won an award? Has any of your staff won awards?

In one of our podcast episodes, Joanna Love mentioned using authority in their marketing,

"We've created a media page. Every time we've been in the media or every time I presented at a conference or one of our staff has done something fantastic. We put it on a media page, and we sell it all the time. So, that shows social proof that we know what we're doing."

You can also highlight things like degrees or special achievements.

For example, one of your team members may be an Olympian or national level swimmer.

Consistency

People like to be consistent with the things they have previously said or done.

If someone verbally commits to something, then they will typically feel a need to stay consistent with that commitment.

In some ways, I feel this is the hardest principle of influence to leverage; however, it can be powerful if the opportunity arises.

An example of consistency can be highlighted via a study that reduced missed appointments at health centres by 18% simply by asking the patients, rather than the staff, to write down appointment details on the future appointment card.

You could apply that same approach in your swim school by getting new customers to agree or commit to certain policies or standards such as acknowledging the importance of at least an 80% attendance record to ensure progression of their child's swimming skills.

If a new customer reads and commits to certain rules they will have a much higher likelihood of staying consistent with that commitment.

Liking

People buy from people they know, like and trust.

This makes it important to train your staff on rapport building skills. If your sales team and frontline staff have good rapport building skills, you will have a much easier time converting your leads into customers.

Simple things like smiling and saying hi can go a long way to strengthening relationships with your customers.

Even the way your staff answer the phone impact the way prospects feel about your business and the first impression.

Consensus

Consensus relates to the principle that people will look to the actions and behaviours of others to determine their own.

For example, when I go to the beach during the summer, we like to buy some ice cream. Naturally, there are 3 or 4 ice cream shops along the street opposite the beach. How do we choose the best ice cream shop? We look for the one with the most people. If it has a line out the front door, then it must be good right!

If everyone seems to be doing it, it must be good right.

We use this principle in our software business, in our newsletter, we do spotlights on new installations and case studies from our existing customer base. We make noise about all the people using our platform, which makes it seem like everyone is doing it!

If we didn't make a noise they may not be aware of all the others using our platform.

You can leverage this principle in your swim school marketing and sales conversations.

If your swim school has a long waiting list and high occupancy levels make sure you make this public.

Include it in your newsletters and conversations with new customers.

These claims must be true.

There are countless ways you can include the influence principle of consensus in your marketing.

If you take the time to understand the 6 principles of interest, you can greatly improve your marketing and improve your sales conversion rates.

In the next chapter, we will explore some more specific strategies for boosting your conversion of leads into new customers.

7

Conversion Boosters To Convert More Leads Into Swim School Customers

If you are not getting the sales results you want, you typically have traffic problems (not enough leads) or a conversion problem (you are not converting the leads you are getting).

I have previously talked about the customer's sales formula - Traffic x Conversion = Customer acquisition.

Now we will explore some ways to improve the conversion of the leads you are generating.

Capture the contact information of your leads.

The essence of direct response advertising is generating leads by getting them to put their hand up and identify themselves.

Many businesses make the mistake of focusing on "branding" as their primary advertising objective. Branding might work for giant businesses with millions to invest in advertising; however, it is usually a bad idea for small businesses.

All advertising investments should be trackable.

If we invest 100 dollars, we should know with some degree of accuracy how many leads that will generate.

We can define a lead as someone who has put their hand up in some way. This could be filling out an online form or walking into the centre.

One of the best things you can do to improve your sales conversion is to capture the contact information of your leads.

By capturing contact information you can continue to follow up and nurture your leads which leads to better conversion.

Web opt-in forms

In the current climate for swim schools, a large number of leads are generated online.

Based on the data we have collected, over 40% of leads are captured online. I would estimate that the number of leads generated online is a lot higher.

People tend to do their research online before acting; they will search google for swim schools in their local area and browse a few websites before taking action.

Many leads that "walk-in" to your facility have likely already researched your facility online.

This makes planning your digital experience and website content very important.

You must have a high-quality website easy for potential customers to navigate. First impressions count!

One of the main goals of a website should be to generate leads in the form of a name and email address.

An email address of a potential prospect is worth considerably more than someone visiting your website and leaving. This is because you can continue to communicate with them, provide them with valuable content and build a relationship with them.

One of the primary objectives of your website should be to capture lead contact information. This is typically done via a form on your website.

You might even offer a "bribe" or something in value in return for the person's contact information. A perfect example of this is by offering a FREE Trial lesson.

Example:

See why our lessons are the best available!
Register for a FREE trial lesson
Name
Email

*Details for your child's trial lesson will be sent to your inbox.

It is also important to think about the positioning of your opt-in forms on your website.

Some swim schools make the mistake of putting an opt-in form on the contact us page or on some other page that is hard to find.

Ideally, your opt-in form should be present on the HOME page of your website and above the fold, so it's visible as soon as the page loads.

Simple things like the placement of your opt-in forms are often overlooked, which can have a dramatic impact on the number of contacts you collect.

For example, in our software business on our home page- the first thing visitors see when the page loads is an option to watch a video demo.

When they click on it, a form pops open, which asks them to enter their name and email address to be emailed a video demo of our software. This allows us to capture the contact information of a lead, which we can then use to follow up with further education and valuable content.

You could argue that if we just put the video on our website without requiring an email opt-in to watch it, it would be watched by more people. However, we are interested in qualified leads who are truly interested in learning more about our software.

Ideally, you want your website leads to drop directly into a CRM (customer relationship management) system that can maintain a database of all your active leads.

Offer a trial lesson

A trial lesson is a great conversion tool to help get digital enquiries into your swim school and trying things out.

A trial lesson gives you the benefit of capturing the contacts email address as well as allowing you to further connect with the prospect when they come into the centre for their trial.

As mentioned previously, the best place to advertise your free trial pass is on your website home page above the fold. This ensures everyone that who visits your website see's this offer.

Use testimonials and social proof

Another great conversion booster is testimonials and social proof.

Testimonials help build trust, authority, and credibility.

Video testimonials are enormously powerful because you can see the authenticity of the person.

I recommend having multiple testimonials in both written and video form in a prominent place on your website.

This will help those prospects that are sitting on the fence and need that little nudge of motivation to take the leap of faith and register for your trial pass or decide to join.

Make your phone number visible on your website

A lot of swim schools make the mistake of making it hard for their prospects to connect with them.

Your phone number should be visible on your websites home page without the user having to scroll. (Top right-hand corner is an ideal spot)

If a prospect has a question you want to make it as easy as possible for them to connect with you.

Yet so many swim schools have their contact number buried on some web page that is exceedingly difficult to find.

If a prospective member can't easily connect with you they may well consider one of the other options available to them in your local area.

Respond rapidly to online enquiries

One of the best ways to convert more leads into customers is to respond very quickly to your online enquiries.

If someone submits a question or enquiry online it's beneficial to respond a quickly as you can. (Ideally within two hours)

A phone call to the prospect is the most personal way to follow up online enquiries and will have the best results.

Make sure you train your frontline or sales staff on the importance of quick follow up.

Use a video sales letter

Your website should be focused on conversion. It's important to make the most of this important piece of real estate by ensuring that every element moves a prospect closer to a customer sale.

One of the best conversion elements to include on your website is a video sales letter.

This should ideally be placed above the fold so the member can see it as soon as they land on the site.

Your video sales letter should show your club as well as explain the key benefits they will get from joining. It should also include testimonials from happy customers as well as a clear call to action.

Video sales letters work best when the owner or manager of the swim school is featured in the video as this creates a personal feel.

The best thing about using a video sales letter is that it can help you say so much more than what you're able to convey on a static web page.

It can help take a prospective member from maybe to a hell yes when done correctly.

Leverage live chat or messenger

Another conversion-boosting tool is using live chat on your website. This allows prospective customers to ask specific questions which, when answered, can help them reach a buying decision faster. We use this on our software website and have found it to be particularly effective.

You can even set it up where multiple team customers can have access so they can take up chats as they come through.

We use and recommend https://www.livechatinc.com/

A similar option that is very powerful is using messenger chat. This leverages Facebook messenger and allows you to engage and follow up with prospects over messenger.

This is another channel that can be used in your marketing efforts.

We recommend using Mobile Monkey for setting up messenger chatbots.

Have a frequently asked question section on your website

A prospect who has un-answered questions in their mind will not act.

To reach the sales we need to overcome any objections.

A FAQ or frequently asked questions section on your website can help answer any unanswered questions in your prospects' minds.

Here are some examples of FAQ's you can include on your website

- When does the swim school open and close?
- What support is open to customers?
- How long does it typically take students to pass through a level
- What facilities are available in the change rooms
- Etc

Leverage consumer awareness content

Another powerful strategy to improve marketing conversion is to leverage consumer awareness content.

This involves creating content that is designed to expose or uncover industry pitfalls and helps educate the prospect and set the buying criteria.

An example of this is from the carpet cleaning industry. Marketing expert Joe Polish used this strategy to go from dead broke carpet cleaner to the top of his industry.

Whilst all other carpet cleaners would advertise their business in the same way (name, phone number etc.) his advertisement was completely different.

It would say...

7 things every homeowner should know before getting their carpets cleaned

This ad would lead to a free consumer awareness guide that the prospect could download which would educate them about things to be aware of such as how different chemicals used in carpet cleaning can be damaging for people with certain allergies or pets or methods carpet cleaners take to cut corners which compromise carpet quality.

This approach allows the business to set the buying criteria through education.

This same approach can be applied to the swim school industry.

For example, you could have an ad that says...

9 things you should know before choosing a swim school for your child.

If someone is actively looking to join a swim school, do you think they will be curious about what these 9 things are before joining your competition?

Using this strategy, you can take the pole position and stand out from your competitors through education-based marketing.

The full dynamics of this strategy are outside the scope of this book however adding a consumer awareness strategy into your marketing mix can lead to a significant boost to your marketing efforts.

Here is a summary of our 9 marketing conversion boosters

1. Capture the contact information of your leads
2. Offer a trial pass on your website
3. Use lots of testimonials and social proof
4. Make your phone number visible on your website
5. Respond rapidly to online enquiries
6. Use a video sales letter
7. Use Live Chat or messenger chat
8. Have a frequently asked question section on your website
9. Leverage consumer awareness guides

8

What Is The Number One Marketing Method For Generating New Leads For Your Swim School?

If you follow the lead generation and conversion strategies presented in the last two chapters, your swim school will see a strong flow of new customer acquisition month after month.

However, if you could only choose one marketing strategy to maximise the success of your swim school what would it be?

In our podcast - The Swim School Business Podcast, we asked our guests what their best strategy was for acquiring new customers to their swim school.

We received a lot of good ideas however one theme was consistent through almost every interview - Word of mouth.

Word of mouth comes from happy and satisfied customers. Typically exceeding a customer's expectations is what helps drive a raving fan who will recommend you to friends, extended family and almost everyone they meet.

Here are some snippets from some of our podcast interviews talking about their most effective customer acquisition strategy:

Episode 24 - Joanne Love - "Word of mouth and social proof is still the best. It's that reputation and letting clients see that reputation.

Episode 30 - Scott Wilson - "What attracts customers to our school is its reputation. I think reputation is built a lot on what's the consistent experience our customers receive. If we can make sure that the experience the customer's receiving on a day-to-day basis is consistent and they know what they're expecting, of course, they get results.

Episode 32 - Daniel Fulton- "Word of mouth is huge for us. We do a lot of work with sort of social media and things like that, share our passion for health and just really telling our story to potential customers. How we deliver our swimming lessons, educate people on our program, or introduce our staff telling them a little bit about them personally and lastly, celebrating success."

In our podcast interviewing the swim schools' industries leading operators we asked the question- Do you focus more on customer acquisition or customer retention in your swim school.

We found from their responses that almost ALL leading swim schools focus more heavily on customer retention and creating an exceptional experience for their customers.

This is because it's a win-win.

Focusing more on customer retention not only results in better customer retention results, but it is also the fuel that drives your word of mouth that drives your customer acquisition engine.

Once your swim school business has reached a critical mass of customers- retention should be your biggest focus.

Although the guests on our podcast said that they focus more heavily on member retention, I believe as a whole the industry is not focusing enough on retention.

It's important to remember that our podcast guests are in the top 5% of the industry and the actions that they have previously taken have helped get them there.

As a collective, the industry has some way to go with its focus and approach to member retention.

In a 2021 survey of ASCTA members, it was found that 61.7% of respondents do not measure customer retention.

This presents a significant opportunity for the wider industry to drive significant improvements in their overall performance.

In the next chapter, we will explore specific strategies for improving customer retention and how you can accelerate your results.

9

Foundations Of Customer Retention Success

Before we continue, let's quickly talk about some member retention fundamentals.

Foundations are really important.

Sometimes, I go on holidays on the Gold Coast in Australia. Gold Coast has a lot of high-rise buildings and currently, they are constructing one of the biggest towers ever built there. It is 3 buildings in one called Jewel.

We were staying about 500 metres away from this construction site, and each day we would walk past the site.

They were in the process of building the foundations. What blew my mind was how far they were digging down. They were digging and carrying massive amounts of sand and dumping it onto the beach. The hole they were digging looked to be hundreds of metres deep.

It was amazing to see just how deep the foundations needed to be for this kind of building.

If you want to build something substantial, you need to have strong and deep foundations.

If the foundations are weak or not well established, you will limit your success and the return of your efforts in the future.

If you get the foundations of your swim school correct, it will make your job of minimising attrition or churn a lot easier.

So, what are the foundations you need in place to maximising your future retention success?

(By the way, if you're well established, there is always an opportunity to change some of these foundations as most are to do with your belief systems and confidence.)

Be selective with your customers and increase your prices

Think about the type of customers you want!

Some swim schools are opportunistic and desperate when it comes to acquiring customers.

You want to be more selective when it comes to the type of member you attract.

A fundamental strategy I recommend is to raise your prices.

This helps with attracting a higher quality of customer who is less conscious of price and discounts and more focused on the *value and results* they receive.

You can always start with a small increase in pricing and test the waters. You will most likely find it has little impact on your customer conversion rates.

A lot of swim school owners will argue that they can't raise prices because their competitor down the road is charging less. This attitude is flawed in many cases. Your focus should be on delivering higher levels of value to your existing customers and creating a community. If you charge too little, you cannot create that value and positive environment. Position your swim school as a high-value community where positive results and progression are achieved.

The worst thing you can do when running a swim school is to enter a pricing war with competitors. It is a no-win game that only ends in tears. Focus on charging higher prices and delivering exceptional value that makes those prices a great investment.

Charging higher prices is another way to filter out the wrong type of customers and only attract the type of customers more likely to convert into long-term customers. This one strategy only can almost have an instant impact on your attrition rates.

Play the long game

Yes, we want results quickly. However, retention can be both a short term and long-term game.

The biggest gains will come in the long term. However, small improvements can lead to significant gains in the long term. This is particularly true for larger clubs with over 1000 customers.

A one or two per cent improvement in annual retention rates can result in a difference of hundreds of thousands or even millions in the long term (5 years and beyond).

The same applies to our decision making. We want to make decisions for the long term.

If you attempt to take shortcuts to get quick wins, this may give your revenues a quick spike; however, this is like having a hit of sugar that spikes quickly and leaves you feeling flat and lethargic.

Make retention a priority.

Retention mirrors the results you can create or deliver for your customers. This is what your customers are buying from you. They are buying a result to see their child progress and develop skills that will keep them safe in and around water.

Ask yourself the question...

What if you only got paid based on your ability to produce a result?

Would your family go hungry, or would you thrive?

Would your actions be different if you were only paid on your ability to produce a result for a customer?

 I bet a lot of staff would be a lot more attentive and supportive of customers if they were only getting paid based on a result.

This is the attitude we should have and attempt to install through the culture of our swim school. Your staff should be passionate about helping customers and their children get results.

Your attrition rate is our scorecard for how well we have been able to deliver a result to our customers.

If you can make your culture about serving customers and helping deliver results, your retention results will largely take care of themselves.

Invest in customer retention

I was recently talking to a very successful business person who runs a customer/subscription type of business.

He has been running this business since 2002 and has had success across several international markets.

In our discussions, he mentioned that he hired "customer success" based staff at a ratio of 2 to one for every salesperson. This means that for every 1 salesperson, he has 2 customer success staff.

It is little surprise they have very loyal and long-term customers with an almost non-existing annual attrition rate.

He understands the importance of customer retention. It not only makes sense when you look at the mathematics, creating happy customers and raving fans also has a positive impact on word of mouth and referrals, which is why he doesn't need to employ as many salespeople.

Many swim schools focus the bulk of their efforts on customer acquisition and invest little in customer retention.

If you look at the KPI's and metrics that most swim school managers track, most are sales and revenue-based.

Where you focus is where you get results. If you want to improve retention rates at your swim school, the best place to start is by giving it more focus and more resources.

Larger customer base = Bigger impact

An important thing to understand is that attrition rates or what some people call "churn" becomes more of a factor for swim schools with larger customer bases.

Here is an example outlined in the Customer Economy Book by Robbie Baxter:

4% churn for a small school generating 10,000 per month in recurring revenue.

This means you are losing 400 dollars per month. For example, (for simplicity) if you are charging each customer 100 dollars per month for their customer, that means you would need to acquire 4 new customers per month to maintain your current revenue.

Acquire more than 4 new customers, and your revenues are growing! Easy huh!

If we compare this to a larger swim school:

4% monthly churn for a centre generating 100,000 per month in revenue. Now you are losing $4000 each month based on your churn and need to find 40 new customers just to maintain your current customer.

Finding 40 new customers is a little trickier than just 4.

And that's just to maintain your current revenue and not grow!

As a swim school owner, this should be a little scary. However, it gets worse...

Diminishing returns on customer acquisition:

Because you need to continually acquire new customers each month to replace those that you have lost, if you have a high churn rate, you will quickly burn through all of your prospective customers trying to acquire a large number of new customers you need to maintain your revenues.

In any market, over time, your offer and ability to acquire new customers/customers becomes more difficult.

This is because you start with a bunch of prospective customers in your local area. This group of prospects is not infinite.

Over time most people in your area will become aware of your swim school through your various marketing efforts. Some join, some join and quit, some already know about you and have decided they are not interested, some are happy at another swim school.

The longer you have been in a market, the harder it gets to continue to acquire a high number of customers. Yes, new people come into the area and there are new children born each year but not at the rate required to continue to fill your pipeline effortlessly.

This means if you continue to have high attrition rates, you are essentially a ticking time bomb.

As it gets harder to acquire new customers, suddenly, your customer numbers start decreasing at a rapid rate.

Does this sound familiar?

Many learn this lesson when it is too late, and they are in a world of pain.

By understanding the importance of retention and giving it the attention, it deserves, you put yourself in a position to maximise the success and profitability of your business.

You can't control the uncontrollable

You cannot completely stop attrition.

Some customer churn is completely out of your control. People move areas, move jobs or sometimes even pass away.

So don't beat yourself up about not having a 0% attrition rate. Accept that you will always have some churn. It's the controllable attrition we want to limit and focus on.

Start your customer retention journey here!

There is one thing you should do before you act on improving your retention results.

Before starting any journey, it's important to know your starting point. You need to know what your current retention performance looks like!

How else would you know if the strategies you are implementing are working or not?

Although almost every swim school owner and manager understand the importance of customer retention, a staggering number does not consistently measure it.

This is non-negotiable. It needs to be measured and tracked every month.

If I ask, you should be able to tell me your retention results for a given month in the past.

If you take just one action from reading this book, it should be to measure your retention performance each month.

What gets measured improves because you are focusing on it.

If you just do this, you will see improvements!

What is the best way or formula for calculating member retention?

Unfortunately, there is no clear-cut best answer.

There are several metrics and formulas for calculating retention rates, which all have their pros and cons.

Common methods include calculating monthly attrition, the average length of stay and annual retention rates; however, the most important thing is that you are tracking something!

Below are some of the best metrics for calculating member retention rates.

Metric 1 – Attrition

Many facilities calculate attrition as a baseline for success. Attrition is measured by taking the number of cancelled customers at the close of each month and dividing this by the number of active customers from the beginning of the month and multiplying by 100.

Attrition = (Cancelled Customers / Month Starting Customers) x 100

Typical rates here are 2-4% (If you have a 5% monthly attrition, this means you are turning over more than half of your customer base in 12 months, which is not good). Ideally, you want to be aiming for less than 3 as a baseline. (2% should be your aim)

Metric 2 – Length of stay

Another commonly used indicator of retention is to calculate the average length of stay (LOS) for a member.

Divide the total number of months your customers stay by the total number of customers to get the average number of months that a member stays.

Length of Stay = Total Months Stayed / Total Number of Customers

Note – this number can be misleading because your long-term customers skew the result as artificially higher.

The easiest way to calculate this is to get a spreadsheet with all your customers and their customer start date.

Create a column for the length of the customer. (Ideally, your customer system has this metric already). Total the column in excel for months stayed to get a total and then divide that by your total customer base.

Metric 3 – Annual Retention Rate

Retention rate is the number of customers you keep over some time, i.e., 12 months.

Steps to calculate the annual retention rate:

1. Make a 12-month chart and record: Starting several customers for each month from Jan to Dec.
2. Total the beginning number of monthly customers (overall 12 months) and divide by 12 to calculate the average beginning monthly customer.
3. Total the number of cancelled customers divided by the average beginning monthly customer to get your attrition.
4. Subtract from 100

E.g., If your average beginning monthly customer was 1,523 and you had 576 customers cancel over 12 months

576/1523*100 = 37.82% annual attrition

100 -37.82 = 62.18% annual retention rate

Consider setting up a spreadsheet or google sheet to collect these key data points, such as month-end customer and total cancellations for the month.

Set a reminder in your calendar for the 1st day of each month to record this data for the previous month.

If you are a busy manager, schedule this as a task for one of your team customers.

We use a tool called Asana for scheduling team tasks, which can be set up repeatedly, which works great for helping team customers stay organised with these sorts of tasks.

I suggest recording all 3 metrics as all 3 have their pros and cons.

The monthly attrition helps keep your finger on the pulse each month, and you can react or identify any cause if a poor month takes place.

You can also take this data further...

For example, you may look at different customer segments or programs and the effect these have on the average length of stay.

For example, you could compare customers in specific levels and compare the average length of stay between those groups.

This more in-depth analysis can help you identify drivers of retention.

Once you understand what leads to improvements in customer retention, you can then structure your programs and process to maximise these drivers.

The three key ingredients in your retention recipe

If there is one area that swim school managers find most challenging it is member retention.

Almost all swim schools struggle with it.

It's one of those things that can be extremely complex yet simple at the same time.

Let's try and simplify things for a moment.

Retention strategy can be divided into three core areas.

These 3 ingredients must be in place for having a strong customer retention result.

Ingredient 1 - Onboarding.

Onboarding is the action you take to help get new customers started.

Half the battle is overcoming the inertia new customers face.

First impressions count and a good onboarding process help set the foundations for a new customer to maximise the value they receive from your service.

A classic example of where onboarding is used well is in the online software industry.

If I buy an online software or tool to use in our business, I will likely receive several emails, videos, phone calls, etc., over the first weeks and months of using the service.

These software providers know the importance of educating clients to help get them a result or value as quickly as possible.

The same applies to the swim school.

How can you help your new customers get value or a result as quickly as possible?

How can you help set expectations with new customers?

Your onboarding should be a pre-planned and automated set of communications or touchpoints with customers. Every piece of that content should be strategically planned for maximum impact.

Ingredient 2 - A system to deliver a result (Progression)

The next vital ingredient in our retention process is a system to deliver a result.

Your results are the progress of a child in their ability to swim. In essence, your lessons are your system to deliver a result. However, this is a simplistic way to look at it.

Here are some other considerations in your ability to deliver a result.

1. Are your teachers good at making lessons fun?
2. Are your teachers good at keeping children focused?
3. Is the experience pleasant for customers?
4. Do parents receive feedback about their children?
5. Do parents have clear expectations?
6. Do you have a process to identify struggling students?

Your process to deliver a result is made up of many little things.

Ingredient 3 - Interaction/Communication

The social element of the swim school is critical to its feel and culture. Customer interaction and communication has a huge impact on customer retention rates. That's why it's important to train your staff on how to effectively interact with customers.

It's also important to schedule time that is dedicated to interacting with customers to ensure that it gets done.

A swim school should feel like a community, and this is very much driven by its culture and the way staff interact with customers.

By including these 3 vital ingredients in your member retention strategy, you will maximise your chances of retention success.

Let's break down each of these key areas further and look at the specific strategies we can employ to enhance our outcomes.

Onboarding - How to jump-start your new customers

Onboarding is helping new customers get started in your swim school.

An effective onboarding process should include a variety of different communication channels, including email, SMS, video, and human to human communication.

The content in your onboarding process should educate new customers and help them get value.

One mistake a lot of businesses make is that they under-communicate with new customers.

They don't want to be pushy or annoying.

The key is to communicate with helpful and engaging content.

People are turned off by too promotional content, not by helpful educational content.

Another important consideration is communication cut through. You are fighting for attention with all the myriad distractions in our daily lives.

It's also important to consider that a typical email open rate is around 30%. This means if you send your new customers 3 onboarding emails, likely, they will only open 1 of these.

We recommend having somewhere between 7-11 onboarding touchpoints with new customers in the first 30 days and to ensure these include a variety of different media (some emails, SMS, phone, video, messenger chat).

Online based subscription companies such as software providers are very good at onboarding because they know they must get a new customer engagement and getting value from their service as quickly as possible.

If a new user doesn't use the service in the first few weeks, they are unlikely to remain a customer for long. The same applies to the swim school, we need to do everything possible to ensure our new customers build momentum and see progress quickly.

A good onboarding strategy can often set the foundations of regular attendance which is another pillar of customer retention.

An onboarding sequence of communications is not about just touching base with your customers, it's about education, setting expectations and building a relationship.

Powerful ideas for developing an effective onboarding process at your swim school

Let's explore some ideas for developing an effecting onboarding process for your new customers.

Welcome email/video

A welcome email should re-sell the benefits of your swim school as well as the available resources to support the customer on their journey. A video format can be good as this adds a human touch, which can increase connection and rapport with your customers.

FAQ

FAQ stands for frequently asked questions. If a new customer has never been to a swim school before, they are likely to have a lot of questions. Eg. How often can I expect feedback about the progress of my child? Or What is the makeup lesson policy etc.

By having a FAQ in your onboarding sequence, you can address any common questions and misunderstandings that can cause a roadblock for customers.

Roadmap

Give customers a clear roadmap- Map out the recommended steps to success they should take.

For example, a road map might look like this.

5 steps to maximise your child's success in our program

1. Set up your parent portal- Instructions here
2. Expect feedback every 90 days
3. Report absence before lessons to claim makeups

4. Maintain an 80% attendance rate
5. Discover what your child will be learning

Quick wins

The concept of quick wins is a powerful tool in your onboarding arsenal.

Essentially you are asking, how can we give our customers a quick win? How can we get them a quick result?

What is a basic skill you can teach parents that they can practice with their children at home? (In or out of the water).

Little things like this can not only improve the progress of the child but also maximise their engagement in the program

Introduce key staff

A key objective of your onboarding process is to build a connection with new customers.

A great way to achieve this is by introducing key staff via a video.

This may include the key on deck staff, reception team members and owners/managers.

By helping new customers put a name to the faces they see within your centre you are helping break the ice and lay foundations for deeper connections.

Referral/Bring a friend

A great way to increase the lead flow is to promote a bring a friend opportunity to new customers.

Re-iterate this in your onboarding sequence by offering the opportunity for their child to bring a friend to a lesson for free within a certain time frame from joining.

Dialogue

Consider asking each new customer if they have any questions?

Often, if customers have a question, they won't ask to avoid embarrassment.

Be open and invite customers to ask questions. This strategy can help create a dialogue and eliminate any roadblocks preventing the member from gaining momentum.

We use a concept called SPEAR emails to open a dialogue.

SPEAR stands for short, personal, expecting a response.

Here is an example of a SPEAR email you can include in your onboarding after 2 lessons:

Hi Amy,

How is Jess enjoying here lessons so far?

Are there any questions we can assist you with?

Warm regards,

Swim School

An unexpected gift

Another thing to consider in your onboarding is to add some level of personalisation and wow.

This can be done by things like an unexpected gift or personalised video.

For example, you may bring a brand new customer a FREE coffee as a little thank you for enrolling their child.

This little gift creates a WOW experience that will help optimise their experience.

Another way to create personalisation and wow is by doing a 30-second personal video. This can be done using tools such as Bonjouro app that allows you to create personalised videos quickly and easily.

Essentially you just record a quick welcome message for new customers.

For example, Hey John just wanted to say hi and welcome you and your family. We are excited to have you onboard and are here to help. We will be sending you some cool content over the coming weeks to help inform you about our program and how we maximise the swimming skills of your child., so keep an eye on your inbox for those. Look forward to seeing you in the swim school!

A message like this takes 1 minute to record and send with the right tool. If you have 30 new customers each week, you can expect a process like this to take you 30 minutes to 1 hour each week. An investment that is well worth it in terms of your customer experience and retention.

Most swim schools do a poor job of new member onboarding, a lot have next to no onboarding communications in place, so this presents a huge opportunity to stand out from your competition and improve retention results.

The content you create for your new member onboarding can be repurposed and used in several different areas including on all of your social media channels.

In the next section, we will talk about how we can proactively improve our odds of retention success.

10

The Three Key Ingredients In Your Retention Recipe

If there is one area that swim school managers find most challenging it is member retention.

Almost all swim schools struggle with it.

It's one of those things that can be extremely complex yet simple at the same time.

Let's try and simplify things for a moment.

Retention strategy can be divided into three core areas.

These 3 ingredients must be in place for having a strong customer retention result.

Ingredient 1 - Onboarding.

Onboarding is the action you take to help get new customers started.

Half the battle is overcoming the inertia new customers face.

First impressions count and a good onboarding process help set the foundations for a new customer to maximise the value they receive from your service.

A classic example of where onboarding is used well is in the online software industry.

If I buy an online software or tool to use in our business, I will likely receive several emails, videos, phone calls, etc., over the first weeks and months of using the service.

These software providers know the importance of educating clients to help get them a result or value as quickly as possible.

The same applies to the swim school.

How can you help your new customers get value or a result as quickly as possible?

How can you help set expectations with new customers?

How can you strengthen relationships with new customers?

Your onboarding should be a pre-planned and automated set of communications or touchpoints with customers. Every piece of that content should be strategically planned for maximum impact.

Ingredient 2 - A system to deliver a result (Progression)

The next vital ingredient in our retention process is a system to deliver a result.

Your results are the progress of a child in their ability to swim. In essence, your lessons are your system to deliver a result. However, this is a simplistic way to look at it.

Here are some other considerations in your ability to deliver a result.

1. Are your teachers good at making lessons fun?
2. Are your teachers good at keeping children focused?
3. Is the experience pleasant for customers?
4. Do parents receive feedback about their children?
5. Do parents have clear expectations?
6. Do you have a process to identify struggling students?

Your process to deliver a result is made up of many little things.

Ingredient 3 - Interaction/Communication

The social element of the swim school is critical to its feel and culture. Customer interaction and communication has a huge impact on customer retention rates. That's why it's important to train your staff on how to effectively interact with customers.

It's also important to schedule time that is dedicated to interacting with customers to ensure that it gets done.

I have heard stories from the industry where swim school managers know the name of every child and parent. When your customers are addressed in a personal way they feel like they are part of your community and not just another number.

A swim school should feel like a community, and this is very much driven by its culture and the way staff interact with customers.

By including these 3 vital ingredients in your member retention strategy, you will maximise your chances of retention success.

Let's break down each of these key areas further and look at the specific strategies we can employ to enhance our outcomes.

Onboarding - How to jump-start your new customers

Onboarding is helping new customers get started in your swim school.

An effective onboarding process should include a variety of different communication channels, including email, SMS, video, and human to human communication.

The content in your onboarding process should educate new customers and help them get value.

One mistake a lot of businesses make is that they under-communicate with new customers.

They don't want to be pushy or annoying.

The key is to communicate with helpful and engaging content.

People are turned off by too promotional content, not by helpful educational content.

Another important consideration is communication cut through. You are fighting for attention with all the myriad distractions in our daily lives.

It's also important to consider that a typical email open rate is around 30%. This means if you send your new customers 3 onboarding emails, likely, they will only open and read 1 of these.

We recommend having somewhere between 7-11 onboarding touchpoints with new customers in the first 30 days and to ensure these include a variety of different media (some emails, SMS, phone, video, messenger chat).

Online based subscription companies such as software providers are very good at onboarding because they know they must get a new customer engagement and getting value from their service as quickly as possible.

If a new user doesn't use the service in the first few weeks, they are unlikely to remain a customer for long. The same applies to the swim school, we need to do everything possible to ensure our new customers build momentum and see progress quickly.

A good onboarding strategy can often set the foundations of regular attendance which is another pillar of customer retention.

An onboarding sequence of communications is not just about touching base with your customers, it's about education, setting expectations and building a relationship.

Powerful ideas for developing an effective onboarding process at your swim school

Let's explore some ideas for developing an effecting onboarding process for your new customers.

Welcome email/video

A welcome email should re-sell the benefits of your swim school as well as the available resources to support the customer on their journey. A video format can be good as this adds a human touch, which can increase connection and rapport with your customers.

FAQ

FAQ stands for frequently asked questions. If a new customer has never been to a swim school before, they are likely to have a lot of questions. Eg. How often can I expect feedback about the progress of my child? Or What is the makeup lesson policy etc.

By having a FAQ in your onboarding sequence, you can address any common questions and misunderstandings that can cause a roadblock for customers.

Roadmap

Give customers a clear roadmap- Map out the recommended steps to success they should take.

For example, a road map might look like this.

5 steps to maximise your child's success in our program

1. Set up your parent portal- Instructions here
2. Expect feedback every 90 days
3. Report absence before lessons to claim makeups
4. Maintain an 80% attendance rate
5. Discover what your child will be learning

Quick wins

The concept of quick wins is a powerful tool in your onboarding arsenal.

Essentially you are asking, how can we give our customers a quick win? How can we get them a quick result?

What is a basic skill you can teach parents that they can practice with their children at home? (In or out of the water).

Little things like this can not only improve the progress of the child but also maximise their engagement in the program

Introduce key staff

A key objective of your onboarding process is to build a connection with new customers.

A great way to achieve this is by introducing key staff via a video.

This may include the key on deck staff, reception team members and owners/managers.

By helping new customers put a name to the faces they see within your centre you are helping break the ice and lay foundations for deeper connections.

Referral/Bring a friend

A great way to increase the lead flow is to promote a bring a friend opportunity to new customers.

Re-iterate this in your onboarding sequence by offering the opportunity for their child to bring a friend to a lesson for free within a certain time frame from joining.

Dialogue

Consider asking each new customer if they have any questions?

Often, if customers have a question, they won't ask to avoid embarrassment.

Be open and invite customers to ask questions. This strategy can help create a dialogue and eliminate any roadblocks preventing the member from gaining momentum.

We use a concept called SPEAR emails to open a dialogue.

SPEAR stands for short, personal, expecting a response.

Here is an example of a SPEAR email you can include in your onboarding after 2 lessons:

Hi Amy,

How is Jess enjoying here lessons so far?

Are there any questions we can assist you with?

Warm regards,

Swim School

An unexpected gift

Another thing to consider in your onboarding is to add some level of personalisation and wow.

This can be done by things like an unexpected gift or personalised video.

For example, you may bring a brand new customer a FREE coffee as a little thank you for enrolling their child.

This little gift creates a WOW experience that will help optimise their experience.

Another way to create personalisation and wow is by doing a 30-second personal video. This can be done using tools such as Bonjouro app that allows you to create personalised videos quickly and easily.

Essentially you just record a quick welcome message for new customers.

For example, Hey John just wanted to say hi and welcome you and your family. We are excited to have you on board and are here to help. We will be sending you some cool content over the coming weeks to help inform you about our program and how we maximise the swimming skills of your child., so keep an eye on your inbox for those. Look forward to seeing you in the swim school!

A message like this takes 1 minute to record and send with the right tool. If you have 30 new customers each week, you can expect a process like this to take you 30 minutes-1 hour each week. An investment that is well worth it in terms of your customer experience and retention.

Most swim schools do a poor job of new member onboarding, a lot have next to no onboarding communications in place, so this presents a huge opportunity to stand out from your competition and improve retention results.

The content you create for your new customer onboarding can be re-purposed and used in several different areas including on all of your social media channels.

In the next section, we will talk about how we can proactively improve our odds of retention success.

11 ▋

The Ultimate Retention Plan
For Swim Schools

Retaining your customers is the product of many little things. However, one could argue that the biggest drivers of retention for a swim school are communication and progression.

Did you know that 69% of parent's rate "lack of communication about their child's progress" as the number one reason for dissatisfaction with their current learn to swim provider?

This shows us that parents crave ongoing feedback and communication.

To improve retention, you must improve the way you communicate progress to parents.

Below is a seven-step plan that we have helped hundreds of our clients implement to improve the way they manage progression and retention.

The 7 step swim school retention plan

1. Aim to assess students every 90 days

Parents love regular feedback about their child's progress.

To give them feedback you must first assess their child to gauge where they are in their skill development.

By committing to assess every student in your program at least once every term (90 days), you can ensure that you have something to update parents about!

90 days appears to be the sweet spot when it comes to conducting assessments and providing feedback. Any longer than 90 days and a parent can start to wonder how their child is progressing and any more frequently than 90 days increases the amount of resourcing required to maintain such a process.

Simply assessing each student does not provide parents with any direct feedback. To increase communication and feedback you need a way to translate assessments into communication events.

2. Turn assessments into a communication event

How can your swim school ensure parents receive regular feedback about student progress?

The key is to turn your assessment process into a communication event.

An ideal approach is that a parent receives an email informing them of an assessment immediately after the event.

Our clients do this via our SwimDesk software which helps manage their assessment and feedback process.

The SwimDesk system automatically triggers an email after each assessment.

The assessor can choose between two options

1. Progressed
2. Assessed- Not ready to move up

These two outcomes are linked to specific email templates that inform the parent of the assessment, the outcome and how to find out more.

By implementing this strategy, you will notice an instant impact in terms of parent's appreciation and satisfaction.

3. Decide on your assessment model

Before you commit to a process of providing parents with regular feedback about their child's progress it's important to develop a plan or an assessment model.

Your assessment model is made up of who is responsible for assessments, when assessments take place and your assessment targets.

Who is responsible for assessments?

There are different models within the industry for managing the assessment process. Let's explore the most common...

The Deck Supervisor Model

This is when the swim school employs deck supervisors who are experienced teachers to complete assessments and provide extra support to parents.

By using a tablet, the deck supervisor can input assessment results at the point of a lesson which makes the process efficient.

Employing a deck supervisor can be more costly, however for medium to large swim school the investment is well worth the return in improved customer retention.

Some larger centres will often have two deck supervisors during the one shift who will both have tablet devices.

One of the weaknesses of the deck supervisor model is that the teachers in the pool still need paper class sheets to track who is in their class and where they are up to in terms of their skill progression.

Teachers in the pool using a tablet

A new model that is emerging is teachers in the pool using a tablet. The benefit of this model is that it allows swim schools to eliminate paper class sheets.

Teachers can update attendance and student skill progression in each lesson at the point of the class.

Classes are always changing which means using a paper system can lead to having to constantly re-print or update class sheets.

One downside of this model is the cost. If you have 10 teachers in the pool teaching at the onetime then you will need to buy ten tablets.

The cost of tablets is decreasing which is making this approach more cost-effective.

The important thing to consider here is the time savings of investing in tablets for the teachers. Many swim schools are paying teachers or back-office staff for additional admin time to update paper records into digital. If you pay 10 staff an extra 30 minutes each day to do admin then this expense will quickly surpass the costs of investing in 10 tablets.

The deck supervisors' model is the most common approach we see used within the aquatic industry however a growing number of centres are now implementing tablets for their teachers.

You can also use a hybrid model with both teachers using tablets and deck supervisors who approve final assessments.

We predict over the next 2 years that over 75% of swim schools will move to the practice of teachers having tablets.

When to assess?

Once you have decided who will be responsible for assessing the next step is to decide when assessments take place.

In the industry, there seem to be two approaches

1. Level focus weeks
2. Assessment blitz periods

Level focus weeks are when the swim school will pick one or two levels to focus their assessments on each week. Eg. in Week 2 of the term you may focus on assessing all students in level 8, in week 3 you might focus on assessing all students in level 7 etc.

This approach works well because it gives your team a clear plan to follow, increases accountability and is more consistent in terms of resourcing.

Assessment blitz periods are when the swim school will aim to assess all students in a short period towards the end of a term or period. (Typically, two weeks). The downside with this model is that it leads to resourcing challenges where you need to significantly ramp up your resources during this period to ensure every child is assessed.

From our experience, those swim schools that employ an assessment blitz approach have less consistent results and often fall short of assessing every student.

Therefore, we recommend the level focus week approach or an ongoing model for teachers as the best approach.

Setting goals for your assessment plan

The last step in your assessment plan is to set assessment targets.

By breaking down your overall assessment target into smaller achievable chunks

For example- If your goal is to assess every student every 90 days and you have 1000 students in your program you can break this down into monthly and weekly targets.

In this example (assuming an ongoing assessment approach) your monthly target would be 333 assessments per month and 77.4 per week.

By breaking down your targets into smaller achievable chunks it's easier to monitor your performance and identify if you are falling behind schedule.

The most common reason for failing in the implementation of a feedback process in your swim school is following through and not letting other things get in the way of getting your assessments done.

4. Use descriptive wording when assessing

The quality of your communication comes down to your descriptiveness of the words you use when assessing.

When providing feedback to parents it is important to provide them with as much information as possible about their child's progress. It's not only a matter of saying what skills have been passed, it's a matter of explaining where each skill is in terms of its development, what's improving, what's stagnating and when can they expect their child to progress to the next level.

How do you convey all this information in a way that's easy for parents to understand and not too time-consuming to deliver?

A lot of our clients use a particular model when using terminology for assessing.

Now we recommend this model to every new client we work with because the descriptive grading words provide parents with a crystal-clear understanding of how their child is progressing.

Here it is.

1. Introduced
2. Improving
3. Consolidating
4. Competent

Let's explore this grading model...

Introduced means the skill is just starting,

Next is Improving, which means the skill is improving and might be 50% of the way.

Then, consolidating, means the skill is being put together, it's probably very close, but they are still putting the entire skill together.

Then lastly competent, which means the skill is fully competent and automatic.

The beauty of this model is that it covers all bases in terms of skill progression.

When you use this kind of language when communicating progress to parents, suddenly it becomes a lot clearer to them exactly where the child is at in each skill.

Whereas, if you just had a black and white, competent, not competent, that doesn't tell the parent a lot other than these skills have been passed.

5. Provide parents with feedback via a parent portal or app

Updating parents about the progress of their child's swimming lessons can be time-consuming.

A conversation about a child's progress can take anywhere from 1 minute up to 5 minutes. This is not scalable over 1000 or 2000 children as you don't have the time or staffing resources to complete this mammoth task every term

That's where you need to leverage technology to deliver feedback to parents.

This is what we help our customers with through our SwimDesk platform and parent portal.

A parent portal needs to be very easy for parents to access.

If you don't have the right platform to give parents feedback, and it's hard for them to access you are going to find that the process of delivering digital feedback to parents is too clunky and time-consuming.

Even with the right plan and strategy, having the wrong technology platform for feedback can de-rail your feedback process.

For more information about SwimDesk go to www.swimdesksoftware.com

6. Track non-progression- 30 weeks

Progression is everything in a swim school. That's what parents are paying for.

They want their child to learn how to swim and they want to see that they're getting better.

They want to see that they're progressing in certain skills.

If a parent fails to see progress over a period, the chances of that customer cancelling their child's enrolment increases.

That's why it's important to identify stagnating students in your program and have a special effort to provide them additional support and attention.

We recommend using a 30-week filter and identifying any student who has been on the same level for 30 weeks or longer.

30 weeks is an acceptable time to be able to pass through a level and if they haven't passed it through in that time, we can think, is something going wrong here?

We perhaps want to look deeper into this and we can do some things or take some action to help us get that child unstuck and move through the program.

It might be as simple as assessing that child, it might be that we let the teacher know so that they can spend a little bit more time and attention with that child.

We might even get to the stage if it's 40 weeks, where we offer the parent, a complimentary holiday program or makeup lesson, anything we can do just to show that we are doing everything to help ensure the child is progressing.

Being proactive and on the front foot is the best approach in these scenarios rather than waiting for the parents to get so fed up and so frustrated that they either complain to you or even worse, give you a cancellation notice.

If you could only do one thing to improve your customer retention, it would probably be to identify those non-progressing or stagnating students and focusing more heavily on their development and progression.

7. Track 2-week consecutive non-attendance

One of the biggest drivers of swim school success is attendance.

If a child does not attend lessons regularly, they will struggle to progress from one level to the next.

A student with a poor attendance rate has a higher risk of dropping out of your program.

That's why it's important to identify students who have missed consecutive lessons.

We recommend having an automated "we miss you" email go out after 2 missed lessons and then some more direct follow up after 3 and 4 missed lessons.

The best approach to drive high attendance levels is to implement proactive measures such as educating parents on the importance of regular attendance.

You can also do things like incentives for attendance by offering discounts and prizes for students who have maintained a certain attendance rate over a period.

If you follow the steps outlined in this chapter and make an ongoing effort to ensure they are part of the fabric of your swim school, I promise you you will see some fantastic results in your customer retention metrics.

12

What The Experts Say About Customer Retention

From my interviews with owners and managers on the swim school business podcast, I asked the question - What are the top 3 strategies for improving retention.

Here is a summary of some of the best answers:

Episode 26 - Nick Masson

"The first thing, the most important thing, is fun. If the children and the participants are having fun. If the teacher or the coach is having fun. And if the parents want to interact with the business having fun, then most swim schools can get away with quite a lot, not going well, perhaps in other areas, it just makes it such a more pleasant experience and it keeps them going.

My second thing would be outstanding, high performing teachers. If you've got an outstanding high performing teacher, then my view is that they're like Goldust and do everything to keep them and to get them to mentor and support the teachers around them and to use them as role models.

And the final thing would be the use of high-quality communication."

Episode 30 - Scott Wilson

"Number one, is the child making progress?

Parents need to see it, or they need to be pointed out to them.

Because as we know, in swimming, sometimes there's progress happening in the pool, which isn't quite as obvious to a mom who's sitting on the side of the pool. So, you need to share with a parent. Feedback on progress is really important.

Second, a celebration of successes. I think it's really good to recognize that others know that other children are making progress. Celebrating progress is important.

And third, I don't think you can get away from the quality of teaching.

That's the consistency factor we talked about, but the quality of teaching. That to me comes down to making sure that a good development plan

Episode 12 - Sammy Lawson

"Number one would be a year ago, we started tracking every child who's been in a level for three or more terms.

The support that we give, each term just gets more and more comprehensive as those terms increase. So, if they're on the sixth term lists, they're getting a lot of support from us and a lot of free support.

It's tracking that diligently and providing a lot of communication to parents.

Number two would be to increase the amount of communication we have with people early on, as well as making sure you've got those points of contact early on.

So, we've started calling everyone who joins us from school, welcoming them to see how it's going. We've also started calling people who have left. Now, that's been valuable.

Number three in terms of retention strategies, making sure that the parents know us in some way shape or form. It just feels like they're least likely to leave when it feels like they're at home. I think when you know those people, it changes how you feel about it, and you feel like this is my place."

Episode 16 - Helen Akers

"We have a strategy that we call our guarantee, that each child has been in the same level for two terms or two, and they're on their third consecutive term. We give them extra assistance in the water during the term if they still don't progress to the next level, and then they get a free Express program over the holidays. So, it's either the first week if they still don't progress, or they get the second week for free as well. But to do that, they must stay in a swim school for three consecutive terms and have 90% attendance.

So, that's part of our retention strategy that we work towards to keep our students engaged and involved in their sessions."

13

Little Ways To Improve Your Retention Performance

Often, we focus on some fancy strategy or tool to improve customer satisfaction and retention. However, it is often the little fundamentals that can have the biggest impact on member retention in a swim school.

Here are a few simple ideas to improve member retention in your swim school.

Treat your customers like people

When dealing with hundreds or thousands of customers, it's easy to see a member as a faceless number. Remember, each member is their person with their challenges, emotions and personality. Don't lose sight of the importance of human to human connection.

Appreciate your clients/customers

Thank you notes, thank you gifts for onboarding new clients and/or discounts to your most loyal customers can speak volumes and make a member feel special.

Welcome and ask for constructive feedback

This should include surveys sent by email; however, don't be afraid to ask for direct feedback. For example, how are you finding your time at the swim school? Are you getting the kind of results you were hoping for?

Create a frictionless user experience

Look at your member experience with a magnifying glass and identify any points of friction. Is it hard to sign up, do customers have to fill out heaps of forms? Is it hard to get help?

Invite customers to company functions

Events like breakfasts and information sessions can be a great way to improve member to staff connection in your swim school. Consider holding a small event each quarter.

Treat the act of keeping customers as important as it is to get them!

Results come from where time is focused. If you are focusing more time and energy on member retention, it should improve. Most swim schools do not spend enough time on member retention related work.

Be quick to resolve issues

If a member has a complaint, don't ignore them! Be quick to offer a solution and talk through their frustration.

Keep in touch

This is a big one that we have covered continuously throughout the book. If you do not follow up and stay in touch with your customers, the chances of them dropping out increase, Connecting with staff helps keep customers sticky and engaged, so stay in front of your customers and regularly interact.

Smile and Say Hi

One of the biggest intangible factors in improving customer retention is the relationships you build with your customers. Do your customers feel a connection to your business?

Relationships are built from friendly interaction.

Ensure all of your team go above and beyond to interact and say hi to customers with a friendly smile.

Interact

Schedule time for your key staff such as deck supervisors to directly interact with customers on the pool deck. The more interaction you have with your customers the stronger the relationships will be so make a special effort to interact and connect with your customer.

14

How To Measure Your
Customer Satisfaction

It's always better to know the truth than to put your head in the sand.

That's why it's important to get a regular measure of your customer satisfaction.

The best way to do this from my experience is to use the Net Promoter Survey method.

What I like about the Net Promoter survey is that it allows you to benchmark your performance against previous performances.

How does it work?

The net promoter survey asks customers on a scale of 1-10, "How likely would you recommend "your swim school" to your friends and family?"

The reason for asking this is that we would only recommend things to friends or family we think are good.

If someone scores a 9 or 10, we call them a promoter.

In other words, they actively promote your business through word of mouth.

They are raving fans!

Someone that scores a 7 or 8 is considered neutral.

They are not raving fans, but they are satisfied with your service.

A person that scores 6 or below is considered a detractor. They have some level of dissatisfaction.

The beauty of the NPS survey is that you are left with a result.

Your detractors are subtracted from your promoters, leaving you with a score. This score could be negative if you have more detractors than promoters.

For example, if you had 123 promoters, 69 neutrals and 98 detractors, your net promoter score would be 8.7%.

(Promoters make up 42.4% of responses and detractors make up 33.7%, 42.4-33.7= 8.7%)

A score above 0 is considered solid, whilst a score above 50% is considered excellent.

Here are some NPS scores from well-known companies

1. Apple- 70%
2. Amazon- 69%
3. American Express- 41%

The second step in the net promoter survey is to follow up with all of your detractors by asking them...

"What would we need to do differently to get a 9-10 from you in the future?"

This allows you to identify areas of improvement that you can proactively act upon.

The NPS is powerful because it drives a culture of ongoing improvement and allows you to measure when you improve.

Sometimes companies can put their head in the sand and not survey their customers because they don't want to face the truth.

I have been in that boat. I hate getting negative feedback from customers, so in the past avoided doing things like the NPS out of the fear of getting some negative feedback.

You are better off hearing the truth than ignoring it.

I recommend conducting an NPS survey with your customers every 6 months as this will help you to monitor your customer satisfaction as well as generate ideas for ongoing improvements.

15

Your Team - How To Get The Most Out Of Your Biggest investment

Is A-grade talent needed to run a successful swim school?

One of the biggest challenges of the swim school industry is staff turnover. Often, the industry is seen as short-term work that someone may take on whilst at university or before they find serious work.

This can be problematic because with high staff turnover comes high customer turnover.

Staff build up what I call relationship equity with your customers. When they leave that equity can vanish.

That's why it's important to try and hire for the long term and to provide clear avenues for career growth and advancement.

You do not need a team full of A-players to run a highly successful and profitable swim school.

However, you do need to make the right moves with your team.

Here are 3 common mistakes that centres make when hiring.

3 hiring mistakes that swim schools make:

1. Hiring based on technical knowledge only

A lot of swim school managers look for technical skills and knowledge when hiring. They might find someone who knows everything there is to know about the different strokes and swimming skills and think, "I have found my perfect candidate," but this can often be a mistake.

Customer retention comes from relationships. The connection between your staff and customers is critical to the feel of your swim school. Therefore, hire people with good communication skills as well as sound technical skills.

Good relationship skills should be the priority when hiring staff. Particularly for your frontline teams dealing directly with customers.

2. Not hiring for the long term

Try and minimise staff turnover. You can't stop it completely; however, there are some things you can do to slow the churn.

For example, look at creating more full-time and part-time opportunities for staff. I know some swim schools with full-time staff who have been in their position for almost 10 years.

It is also important to create a pathway for career advancement.

Can teachers work their way up into a swim school manager position eventually?

Clarify that this pathway exists and educate them on the stepping-stones they can take to get there.

3. Not enough training

From my experience in the swim school industry, I have never seen a swim school provide too much training for their staff.

In my humble opinion, improving staff training processes are one of the biggest opportunities for improvement in the swim school industry.

Training your staff has a massive return on investment. It leads to better customer experience, better retention rates and a host of other benefits.

On average, the Fortune 100 'Best Companies to Work For' list provide 73 hours of training for full-time employees, compared to 38 hours delivered as standard practice by others.

The top organisations also had 65 per cent less staff turnover than other organisations in the same sector – partly due to their employee development programmes.

These stats illustrate the power of training.

Earlier, we talked about focusing your time on "high leverage activities", training your team is exactly that.

There are two keys to success when training your staff, having a training manual and scheduling regular training sessions.

Having a training manual

A training manual contains training content and exercises that can train new and existing staff.

In his book- *The Ultimate Sales Machine*, Chet Holmes talks about training his team. He had a training manual with 10 training modules that broke down the key processes within their company.

For example, one week may have been on handling telephone sales where they would review the content and role-play different scenarios.

The next week they might cover how to upsell clients into higher-value purchases.

Roleplay can be extremely effective in helping staff retain training information.

Each week they would focus on a different training module until they had completed all of the modules.

What would they do when they had completed them all? Start again!

Repetition is the key to all skills.

Holmes would have his team so well drilled they could fall out of bed during the night and be able to recite the 6 questions to ask prospects during a sales conversation.

When your team is that skilled, you create a consistently excellent experience for your customers as well as optimise every leverage point available in your business.

Scheduling your training

The other key to a successful training program is locking it in your calendar.

If it's once a month or once a week, make sure it's locked in your calendar, and that staff are expected to attend. (This can be tricky when you have a casual workforce but don't let this be an excuse for doing less training than you should).

You could also record each training session so staff that cannot attend can watch it later.

If you make training your team a priority, you will be rewarded many times over with increased performance.

16

Tips For Improving The Performance Of Your Teachers

The quality of your swim school is very much determined by the quality of your teachers.

Are good teachers hired? or are they developed through the right training and processes?

We explore 3 ways to improve your swim school teaching performance so you can deliver outstanding service to your customer base.

Assess the teachers

In a swim school, we are used to assessing the students however how often do we assess the teachers?

A number of our clients take the time to assess the performance of their teachers.

A more senior staff member will actively watch one of their lessons and evaluate the teacher's performance against performance criteria.

Some clients even use our software to create a specific teaching performance checklist and assessment form to check off for teachers.

Assessing your teachers provides two important benefits.

1. People respect what you inspect - In other words - If a teacher knows they will be assessed from time to time they will make sure they are always delivering their best effort when teaching.
2. Feedback and identification for improvement - By doing a visual assessment of a teachers class you can provide constructive feedback on how they are going and any areas that they can improve upon.

Regular training

Regular training can be hard to fit into the already busy schedule of a swim school however it is well worth the investment.

Consider developing a training plan and schedule that is fixed and that staff are encouraged to attend. You may order some pizzas or have a morning tea with cake and doughnuts to make it more of a team bonding experience at the same time.

You should develop 5-7 key points or principles that all staff should know such as smiling during a lesson and making it fun as well as more specific technical aspects.

These principles should form the foundation of your assessment criteria that we mentioned earlier in point 1.

Measure performance

The last tip for improving the performance of your teachers in the swim school is to measure their performance.

In a medium, to large swim school, it is difficult to monitor the teaching performance of every teacher. That's why it's important to rely on data to monitor the ongoing performance of teachers.

We recommend that our clients measure two aspects when it comes to teacher performance.

1. Progression
2. Retention rate

Progression is measured by how many students progress to the next level under the teacher's guidance. For example, if Sue had 120 of her students assessed in the last two months and 60 progressed to the next level her progression rate would be 50%.

Typically we would want to see a progression rate of around 25% or better over the long term.

It would be worrying to see a teacher have a 5% progression rate over 6 months because it means that a lot of their students are not moving up.

This data may need to be taken with a grain of salt because other factors can be at play such as a specific level has a longer progression time or a particular teacher has a lot of new students. The data simply gives you some information that you can use to explore deeper and see if a particular teacher needs some more training and guidance.

We also encourage our clients to measure student attrition for teachers. Retention directly impacts your bottom line so if a teacher has a high student dropout rate this is a red flag.

Measuring progression and retention for teachers is simple using our SwimDesk software for swim schools. You simply select a date range and click a button to see a detailed report on the performance of each of your teachers.

By ensuring your teaching standards remain high from week to week and month to month you can ensure your customer is receiving outstanding service which will directly impact your customer retention and bottom line.

17

Deck Supervisors - Are They Worth The Investment?

Many swim schools employ deck supervisors as part of their swim school to assist in serving customers – In this chapter, we explore if deck supervisors are worth the investment.

In our observations, swim schools that employ deck supervisors far outperform swim schools that rely on having in pool teachers only in terms of customer satisfaction and retention.

The problem with just having in pool teachers is that their sole role is to teach. They do not have time to help parents find their child's class or answer too many in-depth questions about a child's progress. This is where a deck supervisor can be a great investment in terms of customer service and retention.

The key is ensuring the deck supervisors time is used effectively.

The deck supervisors key role should be to improve levels of customer service and experience. This is achieved by activities such as helping parents find their child's class, assessing students, answering questions from parents and general interactions with parents.

However, it is easy for deck supervisors time to be misused with less productive activities.

At the end of the day, the deck supervisors role is to keep the customers (parents happy). This can be a challenge because a supervisor only has a limited time to keep hundreds or even thousands of parents happy.

For example, if too much time is spent on orientating new students, less time is available to assess and provide communication to parents. That's why it's important to consider ways to optimise the schedule and time allocation for your deck supervisors. You may make it simple and easy for parents to locate their class by creating a colour code system and a place where parents can see what class colour their child is in. This takes the load off the deck supervisor so they can invest their time in more productive initiatives.

We have seen some swim schools where deck supervisors are even responsible for managing new enrolments and time changes. This can be a bad strategy because most of their time gets eaten up on these admin-level tasks which leave little time remaining to focus on customer service and satisfaction. Leverage your reception and admin teams to manage these admin-level tasks and protect the availability of your supervisor.

What should be the main roles of the deck supervisor?

Below is a summary of the main tasks of a deck supervisor and where their time should be invested.

Deck Supervisor workload

Talking to/assisting parents - 30%

Assessing – 50%

Admin/Reporting - 15%

Other – 15%

At the end of the day, the role of the deck supervisor is to improve customer experience and improve retention by connecting with customers and helping address their needs and concerns.

How many deck supervisors do you need?

Employing deck supervisors needs to make financial sense. In other words, they need to have a positive return on investment in terms of higher customer retention rates.

There is no concrete answer to the ideal number of deck supervisors to have in your swim school.

When we ask our clients are they worth the investment the answer is always the same - A resounding YES.

One quick way to roughly calculate the number of deck supervisors you may need is by calculating the amount of assessment time needed to assess all of your students.

We recommend that each student is assessed every 90 days.

Based on this target we can calculate the rough time investment required to hit this target.

For example...

If you had a swim school with 2000 students, assessing each student once every 90 days would equate to a requirement of 666 assessments per month.

Assuming a typical deck supervisor can assess 15 students per hour, this would equate to a time requirement of 44.4 hours per month in assessment time.

As outlined earlier, we recommend that deck supervisors spend half of their time on student assessments which means we would multiply that 44.4 hours per month by 2 to get 88.8 hours per month.

If we break this down to a daily figure (assuming 5 days per week) it would equate to a requirement of approx. 4 hours. This may mean 1 deck supervisor employed each weeknight for 4 hours or perhaps you double up on busy nights.

Again, these are rough estimates and the most important thing to consider is if the investment makes financial sense in terms of a return. (Higher customer retention)

In summary, a deck supervisor can be a great investment for any swim school that wants to maximise customer service and retention. However, you must maximise the return on this investment by ensuring the supervisor is focusing on their core role of serving the customer. This becomes a lot easier when using the right kind of systems and technology to ensure each parent stays up to date with their child's progress.

18

Systemise For Success

Your swim school is one big system

It is very difficult to scale a business without systems. You cannot support a large customer base if your systems are poor and not well defined.

Essentially, your swim school is one big system with lots of moving parts that's goal is to create a happy and profitable long-term member.

This larger system comprises several smaller processes or systems.

W Edwards Demming was an American who moved to Japan and became the father of the quality control movement, which helped Japan rise to economic power after the war.

He said, "If you can't describe what you are doing as a process, you don't know what you're doing."

If you have no process in your business clearly outlined and documented, you have a lot of inconsistency and a lot of variation.

Most swim schools fail to improve customer retention rates and grow their customer base because of a failure of implementation, and that stems from a lack of systemisation.

"Process, not the people, are the key to error-free performance."

"In a business when there is something that doesn't get done or there is a problem more often than note it's a process problem, not a people problem"- Dr .H James Harrington

Yes, having good people is important; however, strong processes and control around those processes ensure that your team, regardless of ability, all consistently produce excellent outcomes.

According to Joseph Duran, 85% of all quality problems result from processes in place, not because of the people who operate within the processes.

"Processes left unregulated will change, but that change will be for the convenience of the people in the process rather than in the best interest of your company or the customer."

The key message here is that most poor performance in business is due to poor systems and poor regulation of those systems.

This makes sense because most health club managers and owners spend little time working on this vital area. This is the "working on your business" that Michael Gerber talks about.

The best example of this is McDonald's.

Everything in McDonald's is systemised and documented.

They have refined their systems over many years and they deliver super consistent results. It may not be the best food in the world, but you consistently get the same output when you get a meal from McDonald's, the fries always taste the same, as do the nuggets or burgers.

The reality is the staff at McDonald's don't particularly have a high level of skill; most are 16 or 17-year old kids working their first job.

The quality and reliability of the McDonald's systems mean that the output of the system is consistent despite not having A-grade talent.

The same principle applies to your swim school.

Without trying to be rude or derogatory, not all swim school instructors are A-grade talent. Some teachers are amazing; however, some may see their job as a stepping stone to bigger and better things.

If you are relying solely on hiring A-grade talent in this industry you are screwed.

That means your systems are the key to producing consistently excellent results.

Member joins -> (Processes/Systems) = Long-term happy customer

The goal of our system is to create a long-term happy customer

The better your systems are, the greater you're chances of success.

If I asked you to present me with your swim school's procedure manual, would you be able to give it to me within the next 5 minutes?

If the answer is NO, this is one reason you're not performing at the level you'd like to be.

The good news is that once you truly grasp the importance of systems, you can get to work on implementing and refining them in your health club.

The extra good news is that a lot of the content we have already discussed in this book provides some great frameworks for implementing systems in your swim school.

A business lesson learnt the hard way

It's hard to understand the importance and leverage of systems. I know this myself because, for many years, this was a massive blind spot in developing my business.

In the early years in my business, everything was in my head. As we grew and scaled, I needed to grow my team because I was wearing too many hats. I was sales, tech support, graphic design, marketing content, finance, the list goes on.

When I would hire someone, I would tell them how I did the process and then expect them to get on with the job. Often, they would make mistakes, and I would be tolerant and try and take them through how I did the process again.

More inconsistencies would occur, and I would quickly become frustrated and think, "If you want it done right, you might as well do it yourself."

I was blaming the people, not the process and the lack of documentation.

As I pointed out earlier in this chapter, quality issues are almost always related to a lack of documented system/process rather than staff.

I was blaming the staff when it was me who was the biggest issue.

This mental block was harming the growth prospects of our business because if you can't build and rely on your team, then it's very hard to scale.

It all changed when a business mentor explained the importance of systems and the impact, they had on creating his multi-million-dollar business.

He would document what he called SOP's, which stands for standard operating procedures.

Document SOP's to maximise performance

My mentor advised sitting down and identifying systems in your business. Then, one by one, writing out all the steps involved in that process.

Then you would complete that process using the written instructions or checklist and identify any important missed steps or pieces of information.

He would then train a staff member by demonstrating and then providing the SOP document or checklist as a tool for the staff member to follow when performing the task.

Implementing this fundamentally changed our business and our ability to scale. Today, basically everything is documented; each week, we review a process and identify where it can be improved further.

The key is making the time to spend a little time each week working on systems in your business.

Thursdays are my day to work on systems. I spent a couple of hours reviewing a system and identifying ways to make it better.

Another great resource or reference on the topic of systemisation is the book Systemology by David Jenyns

Pro tip-You can use screen recording tools like Camtasia to record screen videos of certain processes and use this in your SOP's for staff.

19

Using Technology To Boost The Performance Of Your Swim School

Technology is a must for any swim school.

Good technology can provide massive leverage and an advantage over competitors.

The biggest challenge with operating a successful swim school is that you must maintain relationships with hundreds and, in most cases, thousands of customers.

Without technology, it is hard to maintain contact and relationships with all your customers.

The right technology can help you engage customers, maintain relationships and reduce staff costs.

Below is a list of technology or software systems that most swim schools should consider

- CMS - Content management system (Your website platform such as Word Press)
- Sales CRM

- Marketing Automation system
- Swim school management software
- Direct debit system
- CCTV
- Accounting system

Not to mention potentially dozens of other little tools and plugins

Although technology can be a massive competitive advantage, many swim schools waste a huge amount of time and energy by making some crucial mistakes with technology.

Let's explore some pitfalls to avoid and how to get the most out of your tech.

3 Tips for maximising the use of technology in a swim school

1. Avoid Searching for the holy grail "all in one" solution

A lot of swim school managers make the mistake of trying to find one software solution to manage all aspects of their facility.

As is evident from the list above, there is a huge number of business systems within the swim school. These systems can be enhanced by using the right technology within them.

The problem with an "all in one" solution is that it does most things "OK," but nothing exceptional.

If you were going into battle, would you want OK weapons and an OK army? When fighting your competition, you want to have excellent technology, as this will maximise your chances of winning.

Adopting a "best of breed" approach allows you to have excellent solutions for all your key business systems.

Because our business is essentially a bunch of smaller subsystems, you must be optimising each system with the best technology.

In our business, we have at least a dozen different software tools and platforms.

Here is just a quick list:

- Xero (accounting)
- Active Campaign (Email marketing and automation)
- WordPress (CMS)
- Lead pages (Website forms)
- Zoom meetings (online meetings/webinars)
- Freshdesk (customer support)
- Asana (Project management)
- Slack (team communication)
- Buffer (Social media management)
- Ezypay (Direct debit payments)
- Vimeo (videos)

Most successful businesses these days will have at least half a dozen different systems and a bunch of other mini tools and plugins.

A lot of platforms can easily be integrated or have API's that allow you to integrate platforms. This allows you to get a seamless technology stack that works together.

2. Employ a technology expert or consultant

So much technology is used in modern business; it can be worth-while to employ a technology expert for your swim school. Ideally, you want an expert that can help you set up new technology as well as integrate solutions.

Your technology expert or consultant may have some coding skills so they can create customisations that can help your software sub plat-forms work best together.

A technology expert can help you get the most of the systems you in-vest in.

In the modern environment, a technology expert is almost the most important role in the business!

It's how you use the technology

Many businesses make the mistake of implementing technology with amazing capabilities but fail to get the most out of the plat-form.

An amazing software will be only as good as what you put into it.

For example, if a swim school has an amazing email marketing and automation system with capabilities to automate a bunch of com-munications with customers but fails to get around to writing the content and email copy to set up in the system, then the system has no real value.

You need to invest the time and expertise into creating the content and "subprocesses" around your technology.

We also notice that our clients often implement our software solutions but do not have the content for the system ready to go.

When this happens, they can often get bogged down in other work and waste 6 months or sometimes longer before they get around to it. This is where employing an expert such as a copywriter or marketing expert to develop your content can be a good investment.

3. Don't lose human to human connection

My last point on technology is that nothing will ever take away human to human connection. Technology should be used to enhance our connection with customers. There is a place for email automation and chatbots, but we should always try to make it engaging and personal.

You should always endeavour to include some human-to-human communication with your customers.

It can be a face-to-face appointment, or a follow-up phone call, just don't lose the human-to-human connection.

The swim schools that can get the balance right and maintain some human connection will be the ones that thrive most.

20

The Most Important Technology Tool For Your Swim School

The most important piece of technology in your swim school is arguably your swim school management system.

This is the software used to run your swim school on a day-to-day basis.

Your swim school management software is the heart of your swim school operations.

The wrong software solution can make running your swim school harder than it needs to be.

The wrong software can lead to time spent on manual and time-consuming tasks which rob you of time that can be spent on growing your business.

The gap between good and poor swim school software can be huge so it's important to make the decision carefully.

This is the point where I am going to do a little self-promotion and talk about our software program-SwimDesk.

Our team has spent the last 6 and a half years working on SwimDesk and continue to update it each month with new and improved functionality.

SwimDesk was born when we were spending time with the manager of a local aquatic centre that had a large learn to swim program.

He was talking to us about some of the challenges he was having in his learn to swim program. He mentioned that parents were frustrated by the lack of communication and feedback they were receiving about their children's progress.

He showed us each teacher had paper class sheets where they would record the skill progression of each child. They were considering developing a process where teachers would write out report cards each term to share with parents however they worked out that the time commitment to do this for a swim school with 2000 students would be astronomical.

From seeing this issue firsthand, we were able to see an opportunity to help swim schools improve the way they provide feedback to parents, and we got busy building an initial prototype.

Once we built our prototype system, we were lucky enough to get another local swim school interested in being our Guiney pigs. This process was valuable because they could tell us what was good as well as where we had missed the mark.

After several iterations, we officially launched SwimDesk in the late stages of 2014. Since then the system has been adopted widely. First throughout hundreds of Australian swim schools and aquatic centres, and then in New Zealand and some parts of Asia. Today our platform is used in 8 countries and continues to grow.

I will leave you with a little bit about SwimDesk below, however, I recommend you do your homework and ensure you spend the time to thoroughly investigate and choose the right software for you.

We offer demo "walkthroughs" at no cost so you can spend as much time asking questions and reviewing the functionality that we offer.

SwimDesk swim school software has been designed to help grow your business by providing you with the functionality and capabilities required to run a modern and industry-leading swim school.

Swim schools turn to SwimDesk when they...

1. Are facing growing competition and need to address poor retention rates
2. Are not satisfied with their current swim school software or want to explore if there is a better solution for them
3. Have parents dissatisfied with a lack of feedback about their child's progress
4. Have a lack of visibility on student progression
5. Have very manual paper-based processes that are time-consuming. Eg. writing out certificates
6. Are wanting to provide the customer with more online options and a better online experience
7. Have a desire to provide a high level of service to their customers

"We get a lot of positive feedback about it. Parents are saying that they're very happy that they can constantly see how their children are progressing for our programs via the parent portal and through the assessment emails."

Do you think overall, SwimDesk has been worth the investment for your centre?

"Oh yeah. 100%."

– Peter G. | Cumberland Council Sydney Australia

What makes SwimDesk the best choice for your swimming lesson business?

From managing registrations and payments to tracking student progress, SwimDesk has a comprehensive feature set that can help your swim school deliver an exceptional swimming lesson's experience for your clients.

SwimDesk has a strong focus on customer retention and has an array of features designed to help improve your customer retention results including our famous progression feedback and skill tracking functionality which makes it easy to give parents regular and highly detailed feedback about their child's progress.

SwimDesk has a beautiful and easy to use interface which has been optimised for all devices. This makes it easy for your staff to use and even easier for parents to use via the parent portal on desktop or mobile. One of the biggest complaints from parents is dealing with hard to use and clunky portals.

SwimDesk has an abundance of smart automation triggers that allow you to automate time-consuming administrative tasks such as class cancellations, class changes, consecutive absences and more.

This helps you save time and effort for your team which can be better deployed on further growing your business.

SwimDesk has powerful online booking and scheduling functionality which makes it easy for customers to manage their bookings via the parent portal including managing level progressions and booking make up lessons. This frees up your reception staff and admin team so they can focus on better serving customers face to face.

SwimDesk has the industries best and most in-depth reporting and analytics that can give you deeper insights into areas of improvement and how to further grow your business.

SwimDesk is robust, secure and flexible. We use world-class security and privacy providers to keep your customer's information safe. We also integrate into a range of payment providers allowing us to cater to a range of payment scenarios and business rules.

By choosing SwimDesk your swim school will run more efficiently, create more delighted customers, improve customer retention, and help you run rings around your competition all with less time and effort.

Key features

- Managing swim school bookings

- Powerful calendar filters for quickly finding the right class

- Book and manage makeup lessons and trails

- Powerful waitlist feature

- Online enrolment forms

- Parents can manage confirmed absences via the parent portal

- Parents can book makeup lessons and other bookings online

- Powerful assessment functionality that has been optimised for tablet devices

- Parent Portal and app provides parents with detailed feedback

- Digital certificates customised to your designs

- The world best reporting to maximise retention and swim school performance.

Our clients enjoy greater peace of mind, less stress and operate with greater confidence because SwimDesk does a lot of the operational heavy lifting in their business.

SwimDesk is trusted by hundreds of industry-leading swim schools. These range from smaller private swim schools with 200 students to large national aquatic centres with over 5000 students.

If you're simply looking for the most inexpensive software to operate your swim school then SwimDesk is not the right fit for you.

SwimDesk is the right fit for swim schools that want to create an exceptional customer experience, who want to maximize their growth and revenues whilst enjoying less stress.

21

Tracking Metrics In Your Swim School To Improve Performance

"What gets measured, gets done" - Peter Drucker

Good reporting and measuring the right numbers are important for any business.

I have found that most swim school owners and managers know what they should be measuring; it's just that they do not measure these things consistently.

I am most likely underqualified to speak about keeping track of numbers and KPI's because it has been (and still is) a weakness.

Over time and through discipline and the right process, I have been able to minimise this weakness.

Below are my thoughts on reporting, including what to report on and how to ensure you have a strong process for reporting.

What to measure?

I have found if you measure too many metrics, it can become over-whelming and you tune out to the numbers.

In saying that, you want to ensure you measure enough of the right numbers to keep your finger on the pulse.

Two types of metrics - Lead and Lag

The book - The 4 disciplines of execution, by Chris McChesney and Sean Covey, explore the concept of lead vs lag indicators.

A lag indicator is something that happens downstream as the result of other actions, i.e., Sales. It is the result of actions that came before it, i.e., Prospecting, advertising, etc.

A lead indicator is an activity upstream that leads to the result (lag indicator). In the case above- The number of sales presentations or prospecting calls may be the lead indicator.

The book suggests that managers should focus more on measuring and improving lead indicators as these are the things we can control.

We can control the number of follow up calls we do, but we cannot control our result in terms of sales. The theory is, if you improve your lead indicators, they will improve your lag indicator. The key is choosing or finding the right lead indicators to measure.

The key is measuring both together as you can identify trends.

For example, you may see that actively measuring and improving the number of interactions with customers on the swim school floor, has a positive impact on your retention rates.

Once a correlation has been established, you know where to focus your efforts.

Here are some metrics you may consider tracking for your swim school.

They have been split into lead and lag categories.

Lag Metrics

Acquisition

- Number of new customers (sales)
- Conversion rate
- Lead source (where your leads are coming from)
- Number of active enrolments
- Occupancy rate

Retention

- Cancellations for the month
- Attrition rate (% of customers each month)
- Low visit customers
- Net promoter survey score

Financial

- Profit and Loss
- Cash in the bank

Lead metrics

Acquisition

- Number of leads
- Number of follow up phone calls
- Number of emails sent to prospects
- Advertising cost per lead or acquisition

Retention

- Number of students assessed/parent feedback delivered

- % of students at 30-week non-progression them

- Number of interactions with customers on the pool deck

I recommend you track these metrics monthly at a minimum to keep your finger on the pulse.

Here are some tips from our swim school experts based on discussions on the swim school business podcast relating to KPI's and reporting.

Episode 5 - Julia Wood

"We use reports from Swimdesk to help us to engage with the customers. We look at things like non-assessment and non-progression. We do look at non-assessment reports because we need to highlight the fact that the child's been in a level for a long period or be that 30 weeks or 40 weeks or whatever it is, and there's always children that slip through the net.

Episode 24 - Joanne Love

"We do set goals, but we set goals that we know that we can achieve. One of the things that we do track is our retention rate. Where are the students, what percentage of students come back? And you know, we can show that to a teacher and just have a little discussion. The other thing is, we always put out a survey, if not once a term, at least every six months to ask parents what they think about us? What could they do better?

Episode 19- Suzette Thomas

"The first one is enrolment. How many students do we have actively swimming? The second number that is pretty important is our lead generation. So, which comes back to our marketing. The third number that's probably pretty important is the conversion or the conversion rate. So, the percentage of how many have been converted into actual enrollments.

Episode 26 - Nick Masson

"We use a combined KPI sheet, which starts at the top and runs down through a list of KPIs. The first one is swim school life. Have you got more swimmers this month than you had last month? Are you growing or shrinking? Next, KPI would be a target to swim school sales. So, what is the number of sales you've going to have to make for the month because you roughly know how many children you are potentially going to lose from the swim? If you want to grow your swim school, the number of sales has to be greater than the number of children that you're losing. The final one I'll give you because we have a huge range of KPIs would be the yield per child. "

Episode 32 - Daniel Fulton

"We track quite a lot now. And we're getting bigger and a lot better at tracking everything at the moment. So, one of the key things that I always get the team leaders to have a look at is just our occupancy. So, making sure so that's just around this sort of, I suppose, making things financially viable, I suppose to make sure that we're not sitting at 50% or anything like that, and we've got teachers doing nothing, is just making sure we're maximizing this space in the classes and the sizes within the timetable

Here are some other tips to help improve your reporting processes:

What gets measured improves

You may have heard the saying that "What gets measured tends to improve". If you measure your cancellation or attrition rate each month carefully, you will find this will improve.

This isn't because of some magical force; it's because when you focus on something, you are more likely to develop plans and actions that lead to improvements in that area.

Don't take your eye off the ball

One mistake a lot of managers and owners make is taking their eyes off the ball. We have all done it (myself included). I was visiting a client recently who had traditionally had solid retention rates.

They mentioned that their retention rates had gone down.

They had recently had some staff changes and stopped tracking an important lead metric over the prior 3 months.

Their activity for this metric had become almost non-existent and the lag results indicated this.

They quickly rectified things by tracking and improving the lead metric.

Get it done for you

One of the biggest things I have learnt for reporting is to get it done for you.

As I said earlier, I was one of the worst in history for reporting and admin tasks.

This can be common for busy owners and managers because they have so much else going on that tasks like reporting get pushed aside or delayed.

It is hard to do reporting retrospectively because it's then too late to take the appropriate corrective action.

I overcame this problem by arranging for my assistant to do my reporting for me.

She gets all the appropriate numbers and puts them into a simple one-page report and then posts it in a Slack channel for me called reporting.

On my calendar, I have time each week (15 min) on a Friday morning designated to check the reporting channel and review important numbers.

If I took the time to collate the reporting information myself, it would take at least a couple of hours and would most likely not get done or done late.

22

Personal Effectiveness - Your Results Reflect You

As a manager or owner of a swim school, you are responsible for the results you get.

Ultimately, in the long run, you typically get the results you deserve.

From my experience, your results are based on the small daily steps you take.

It's kind of like building a house, you start with one brick, and each day if you lay a few bricks, then sooner or later, you are going to end up with a house.

Coming from an athletics background in the past, I have spent a lot of time with elite athletes.

They do all the little things to improve their performance, from recovery to eating right to visualisation. This attitude and mindset to maximising their effectiveness propel them to the top of their field.

If you want to reach the top of the tree in your industry, you will improve your chances if you adopt the same attitude as an Olympic athlete.

Do the little things to maximise your effectiveness, and positive results will flow.

I debated whether to include this chapter because it's not directly related to strategies for growing your swim school however I have found a lot of these ideas helpful in my life and work so I thought I would share.

You are the main driver of success in your business, so the more effective you are personally, the more effective your team and business will be.

Here are 8 tips to improve your effectiveness and productivity

Do an 80:20 analysis on your time

We have already discussed the 80:20 principle in earlier chapters and how our results typically come from a vital few inputs.

The same applies to your time and focus. Some tasks and actions are worth much more than others.

For example, when I started our software business in the swim school industry, one phone call I made resulted in a contract with an organisation that led to millions of dollars in revenue being generated.

The initial phone call took less than 3 minutes to secure an appointment. I purposely targeted that organisation due to its high potential payoff.

This is an example of time well spent and focusing on high leverage tasks. I could have spent that same time ordering business cards or selecting office furniture, but those activities have nowhere near the same level of impact.

Take the time to think through all the activities you do during your week and identify the top 3-5 high leverage activities.

Let me give you a hint- They should involve getting and keeping customers.

Schedule time for high leverage activities

It's one thing knowing where you should spend your time- it's another thing doing it.

For me, I hated doing calls and outbound selling over the phone. I am naturally a more shy and introverted type of person, so calling people on the phone was pure torture for me, yet I knew the importance of doing it.

You may have heard the saying that what gets scheduled gets done.

I have found this to be very true.

Each week I have a routine that ensures I have a focused block of time on my high leverage activities.

For example, every Tuesday morning between 10 and 12:30 am and then again on Wednesday morning would be time designated for my sales calls. During this time, I would purely focus on selling. This would mean I would spend around 5 hours every single week doing phone sales, without fail.

This meant over a year I spent 240 hours on generating opportunities on the phone.

The key is consistently doing that activity every week without fail, and it adds up.

Set a specific day and time each week for that key activity and block that time out in your calendar so it cannot be taken away.

If you follow this advice at the end of the year, you will have spent hundreds of hours on high leverage actions, which will drive your business forward to new heights.

Delegate the rest

We all have heaps to do, which can make it hard to focus on the important tasks.

You may be familiar with the Eisenhower matrix for tasks/activities.

I love this because of its simplicity, but it also illustrates an important point that a lot of the activity and action we do each day is urgent but not important. We are putting out fires and responding to things not moving us forward.

The highest leverage area is typically important but not urgent.

These are things like improving our processes and systems, tuning our sales messaging, training our team, etc.

Yet because they are not urgent, they often go undone. That's why the previous advice about identifying and scheduling your high leverage activities is so important.

To have the space to focus on high leverage activities, you need to become good at delegating.

By handing off lower leverage tasks to team customers or even outsources, you can be free to focus more time on the things that will move your business forward.

I made the mistake in my own business of not delegating things quickly enough.

In the early days, I was responsible for everything, from sales to support and admin. I wore too many hats for way too long.

I had the mindset that "if you want it done right, do it yourself". This kind of thinking can hold you back.

Is Richard Branson handling customer support enquiries for his businesses?

How to delegate effectively

An awesome process I learnt for delegation is from one of my business mentors, James Shramko, and it's called a Task Transfer.

You write down everything you do in your week. Every single little task on sticky notes or a pad.

Then you highlight the high leverage tasks and circle the tasks you would like to take off your plate.

Then you have a task transfer list.

The next step is to write some work instructions or an SOP (standard operating procedure) for that task.

Then delegate each of the tasks on your list to someone on your team or hire an assistant or outsourcer to do the task for you.

Training is the key here, invest the time to train the team member in the task.

By doing this process, I freed up so much of my time, so I can invest more into high leverage activities. My only regret was not taking action sooner!

Install time tracking software

Sometimes we are not aware of our behaviour and where our time is spent.

One of the best things I have done is install time tracking software on my computer, which automatically tracks where my time is spent.

The tool I use is https://www.rescuetime.com/.

This can give you insights into where your time is spent.

For example, one of my past colleagues would use LinkedIn a lot. She would use it to identify leads but often got caught up reading content and wasting time. She was simply unaware of just how much time she was wasting each week until it was being tracked.

I used to handle customer support in the early days of my software business. I was spending around 50 minutes every day handling support tickets.

This added up to over 4 hours every week or 192 hours per year. I could employ someone to do this type of work for around 30 dollars per hour, which would make this activity cost around 6000 per year.

Had I spent those 192 hours on more leveraged activities, it could have been worth 5-10 times the value or even more over the year.

Manage your inbox better

The place where most people waste the most time on low leverage activity is within their email inbox.

We can become reactive to our inbox as it's always adding something new to our never-ending list of things to do.

The biggest mistake people make with their inboxes is having too many emails.

What do I mean by too many emails?

These days we are subscribed to so many emails from online shopping to travel to information, the list is endless.

The best example of this is my wife (don't tell her I said this), she is subscribed to so many online fashion and clothing emails that each day she needs to weed through around 150 emails.

The emails that need attention and action are buried in this mess. So to find the 6 relevant emails in her inbox, she must work her way through the opening and deleting over 100 other emails.

The best advice I can give her is to unsubscribe from as many promotional emails as possible.

Your email inbox is for work.

If you need to set up a separate Gmail account for personal use, do this and filter all your promotional junk mail to this account.

Or

You can filter out promotional emails to skip the inbox and go straight to a promotional folder you can check later.

The key message here is to keep your inbox clean and focused on emails that are relevant and need to be actioned.

There are several great email organisation systems out there that are also worth learning. Most are based around the Inbox Zero concept. (Getting your inbox to 0 messages.)

I use a system based on David Allen's Getting things done book, which organises my emails into those that need action, those awaiting a response, those that have been delegated, etc.

The finer details of this email system are outside of the scope of this chapter, so I won't explain it any further. (I might do a training session on it sometime in the future.)

Passwords

Another massive time-waster in our modern world is passwords.

If you are like me, you will have countless online accounts for different tools and services.

I estimate I have well over 100 online accounts.

This should be the case for business owners and managers as you genuinely should be using several tools and platforms to make your life easier.

Just the basics include an accounting system, an email automation system, a project management system, banking, customer support system, survey system, email accounts, scheduling systems, etc.

Some people use the strategy of always using the same password, but then you are prompted to create a new one as the old one expires-Doh! You then try to create something similar, but soon enough, you can't remember was 99! or 90! or dammit! Time to reset.

I got to the stage where this was almost a daily occurrence until I found a system to solve this common problem.

I now use a tool called Last Pass, which is like a vault that saves all my online passwords.

This allows me to simply click a button, and it will enter my password for me.

Since I implemented this tool, I have never had the problem of forgetting my passwords for different online accounts because this manages it all for me.

You can find this tool here- https://www.lastpass.com

I highly recommend you check it out.

Take regular breaks

Performing at a high level requires clear thinking. You are often solving complex problems that can make you burn out quickly.

This is why it's important to take regular breaks- both short term and long term.

During your workday, I recommend taking a break every 90 minutes. Get up and go outside, go for a walk, do some breathing exercises.

Little things like this can improve recovery. I try and get up and go for a short walk outside twice a day, and I find this has a positive impact on my productivity levels and thinking capacity.

I have also found it important to take regular vacations as this can refresh your mind. I invested in good breaks away (even when I couldn't afford it during the early days of our business) I would often generate great ideas towards the end of the holiday or after arriving back as my mind had time to switch off and unwind.

Time away from work is really important. Four weeks off per year is not much! Consider taking a couple of extra weeks throughout the year, and you will find you can work at a better intensity and with more clarity throughout the year.

Learning/Audiobooks

One thing with the biggest impact on my effectiveness and business has been a commitment to ongoing learning.

This is not just ongoing learning in attending a trade conference once or twice a year. I mean committing to two to three hours every week of learning related to business or personal development.

In the early days of my business, this commitment helped me get traction and build momentum.

I would read books, but mostly I would listen to audio programs.

Having a young family made me very busy, so finding the time to sit and quietly read a book was difficult.

However, I could listen to audio programs and consume learning more easily.

I would listen to audio programs whilst exercising at the swim school or going for a run. I would listen in the car when going to meetings, I would listen on the plane, I would listen when vacuuming, I would even listen whilst mowing the lawns (I would need the volume up full for this one).

I was probably over the top, but I had an unwavering commitment to learning as much about business as possible. I have maintained this commitment for over 10 years now.

Everybody has this free time during the day. Maybe it's during your commute, maybe it's when exercising or cleaning. There is no excuse for a lack of time. The time is there, you just need to do it.

THANK YOU

Thank you for taking the time to read Swim school success.

If you want to find out more about the things I've shared in this book, head to greenedesk.com

You will find some bonus resources and templates there for you to download.

I sincerely hope you got some amazing ideas you can implement in your swim school.

I would love to hear how you go, and any wins you have by following the ideas in this book.

You can contact me via the various channels outlined below.

LinkedIn - linkedin.com/in/greenedesklaneharrison

Email - lane@greenedesksoftware.com

Website - https://www.greenedesk.com.au/

Wishing you great success and happiness,

Lane Harrison

CPSIA information can be obtained
at www.ICGtesting.com
Printed in the USA
LVHW080105161121
703397LV00009B/269

9 780646 848099